SHENSTONE'S
MISCELLANY
1759-1763

SHENSTONE'S
MISCELLANY
1759-1763

NOW FIRST EDITED FROM

THE MANUSCRIPT

BY

Ian A. Gordon

GREENWOOD PRESS, PUBLISHERS
WESTPORT, CONNECTICUT

Library of Congress Cataloging in Publication Data

Shenstone, William, 1714-1763, ed.
   Shenstone's Miscellany, 1759-1763.

   Reprint of the ed. published by Clarendon Press,
Oxford.
   Bibliography: p.
   Includes index.
   1. English poetry--18th century. I. Gordon,
Ian Alistair, 1908-   II. Title. III. Title:
Miscellany, 1759-1763.
PR1215.S59   1978   821'.6'08   78-16381
ISBN 0-313-20591-4

Reprinted in 1978 by Greenwood Press, Inc.
51 Riverside Avenue, Westport, CT 06880

Printed in the United States of America

10 9 8 7 6 5 4 3 2 1

ACKNOWLEDGEMENTS

My thanks are due to the officials of the three libraries in which this work was carried out, the British Museum, the Bodleian, and the Alexander Turnbull Library, Wellington; and to the *Review of English Studies* for the hospitality of its pages. Above all, I am grateful to Professor D. Nichol Smith for encouragement and advice generously given.

       Nos a Musis maria longa
       Nequeunt dividere.

                     I. A. G.

UNIVERSITY OF NEW ZEALAND
   WELLINGTON, 1949

CONTENTS

CONTENTS

viii

CONTENTS

CONTENTS

INTRODUCTION

WHEN Shenstone settled in 1745 at the Leasowes in rural Worcestershire he was not, as has sometimes been held, retreating from the world. On the contrary, he set about creating a world of his own, of an elegance at the same time rural and aesthetically satisfying, which the *beau monde* outside was to learn to appreciate and sometimes to envy. Shenstone's finicky but friendly spirit found three ways of expressing itself. First, the little estate of the Leasowes, with little money but inexhaustible ingenuity and true Augustan elegance, he transformed with the aid of vistas, concealed boundaries, grottoes, rustic seats, and inscribed urns into a *ferme ornée*, creating what was, in a period when sizeable fortunes were being spent on landscape gardening, one of the minor showpieces of England. Secondly, he found expression in the essay and the lyric. These his friend, the printer and publisher Dodsley, gathered together and published in 1764–9, shortly after Shenstone's death. It is not the intention of this essay to add to the comments, from Johnson's down to those of the present day, that have been written on the creator of either the Leasowes or the *Pastoral Ballad*.

Shenstone had a third ambition, of which much less has been written. His real niche in eighteenth-century letters was to be that of the arbiter of taste. The standards he set up were not those prevailing. He deliberately abandoned the London scene and the mental climate of the metropolis, which had so long dominated the writing of the century, and offered in their place rural simplicity and unaffected speech and manners. To express these new standards he turned editor, soliciting copies of verses from his friends and selecting what fitted his purpose. These he gathered together, corrected, amended, and finally edited. Of this editorial work all that has so far been known has been his part in the selection of material for

Dodsley's *Collection of Poems*. From 1750 onwards, as his correspondence makes clear, Shenstone was virtually editor of volumes iv–vi of that anthology, providing Dodsley with edited texts of his own poems and of those of a group of his friends.

In the forties and the fifties of the century Shenstone had in his immediate vicinity a group of college friends (most of them now clergymen), leisured bookish gentlemen and literary ladies. Within easy distance there lived John Scott Hylton, a wealthy dilettante, at Halesowen; the Rev. Robert Binnel, Rector of Newport in Shropshire; the Rev. John Pixell, Rector of Edgbaston, and Miss White who was to marry him; in nearby Warwickshire William Somerville had lived at Edstone; Richard Jago was Rector of Snitterfield; Lady Luxborough lived in rural retirement at Barrels, and a few miles away from her Parson Allen of Spernall; Christopher Wren, the son of the architect, lived at Wroxall Abbey. Somewhat farther off but still within visiting distance were his two college friends, Anthony Whistler at Whitchurch, Oxfordshire, and Richard Graves, Rector of Claverton, near Bath. From Easton Mauduit in Northamptonshire Thomas Percy could, without much difficulty, visit his friend and correspondent at the Leasowes. From the writings of this group Shenstone set himself the task of illustrating his conception of poetry, with its praise of simplicity, pastoral elegance, and the innocent pleasures of the country life.

SHENSTONE'S MISCELLANY

Shortly after he began to provide Dodsley with material for the *Collection*, Shenstone conceived the idea of editing his own Miscellany. Writing to Graves with a request for Whistler's verses, 16 February 1750–1, he says:

> My reigning toy at present is a pocket-book; and I glory as much in furnishing it with verses of my acquaintance, as others would with bank-bills.[1]

---

[1] *Letters*, ed. M. Williams, 294.

Of this pocket-book of 1750 nothing further is known. In 1759, however, Shenstone began again with another note-book, which is now for the first time printed in the following pages.[1]

The 1759 note-book was known to some of his contemporaries. Grainger, the author of *The Sugar Cane*, wrote of it to Percy on 10 January 1759, but preparing to leave for the West Indies, he clearly knew nothing of its contents:

> I presume his Miscellany is to consist wholly of his own things. I long to see it.[2]

On 6 January 1759 Shenstone wrote of it to Jago, asking for contributions:

> I could wish that you would favour me with a copy of your Essay on Electricity, and any new copy of verses of your own, or of your friends. Be not apprehensive: there shall nothing appear in print of your composition any more, without your explicit consent.—And yet I have thoughts of amusing myself with the publication of a small Miscellany from neighbour Baskerville's press, if I can save myself harmless as to expense—I purpose it no larger than a 'Landsdown's', a 'Philips's' or a 'Pomfret's Poems'.[3]

Jago must have replied fairly promptly to this letter: his *Peytoe's Ghost* is the fifth poem to be transcribed into the Miscellany.

The volume is leather-bound and measures about $6\frac{1}{2}$ by 4 inches. It had originally contained 266 pages, and the pages of text are numbered by Shenstone 1–241. Shenstone removed several of the sheets on which he had copied poems which he later decided not to include. The whole Miscellany is copiously annotated by Percy, in whose possession the manuscript was for many years. Preceding Shenstone's title-page are a couple of sheets originally left blank on which Percy has copied an ornate inscription on Shenstone with a note suggesting its authorship ('I conjecture it to have been

---

[1] Cf. *Review of English Studies*, xxiii. 43–59.
[2] Nichols, *Illustrations*, vii. 269.　　　　　[3] *Letters*, 503.

written by Miss Wheatley'). Following the text of the poems there are several blank pages; a ballad copied by Percy; notes by Shenstone on 'verses to be procur'd'; an Index by Shenstone; finally the text that Percy preferred of one of his own poems already copied by Shenstone. The original endpapers, removed for rebinding, have been inserted with annotations by Percy. Two contemporary newspaper clippings containing texts of poems copied into the Miscellany are pinned in. The volume is written in ink in Shenstone's hand. Percy's notes are mainly in ink—occasionally red— but in some places are in red or in black pencil.

The Miscellany contains between ninety and a hundred poems transcribed at various dates between the early months of 1759 and the month of Shenstone's death, February 1763. The terminal date is provided by a characteristic note near the end of the manuscript in Percy's hand:

> The Lines in the preceding Page were written a very few days before poor Mr. Shenstone's death, and even after he began to droop; as appears from the Traces of the Letters, not so fair or legible as his usual writing. Being published in London, only 25th January, it could hardly reach Shenstone before the 27th and he died on the 11th February, 1763. P.

Between these upper and lower dates many of the transcriptions can be pretty accurately dated by reference to Shenstone's letters.

HISTORY OF THE MISCELLANY MANUSCRIPT

The manuscript of the Miscellany had many vicissitudes. A bound-in letter from John Scott Hylton to Percy at Easton Mauduit provides the first piece of evidence:

> Mr. Hylton's compliments wait upon Mr. Percy, hopes he receiv'd his letter of the 19th or 20th Instant, and that the herewith inclosed M.S. vol. of Poems will come safe to his Hands.— Mr. Percy will observe that the pages 29–30–31–32–89 and 90 are torn out; probably by design, as containing pieces which Mr. S. might think proper to reject, upon a subsequent perusal. Mr.

Hylton had no opportunity of sending the Book till last week, else it would not have been deferred till This—

Lapall House,
26th June, 1763.

The manuscript remained in Percy's possession until his death in 1811. Probably ignorant of his friend's thoughts of publication, he made no approach to Baskerville. Though Shenstone had included in the Miscellany a selection of the ballads which Percy was to publish in the *Reliques* in 1765, several of them in texts which he specially prepared for Percy's use, the volume had all the appearance of one of the many eighteenth-century commonplace books written for the private entertainment of their owners. But if he did not publish the manuscript, Percy edited it with care, annotating the ballads and adding explanatory notes on contemporary verses, in particular editing with scrupulous care the poems of his own which were in the collection.

In 1780 Percy's library was burnt. The Miscellany's charred edges and texts, often defective at the ends of lines, are sufficiently eloquent. Percy had the manuscript carefully rebound, even having bound in the remains of the original endpapers, on the first of which he wrote:

This precious ⟨word erased⟩ of my poor friend Shenstone was thus piteously burnt in the fire which consumed my Library at Northumbd. House in 1780. P.

On Percy's death in 1811 the manuscript passed to his daughter, Mrs. Meade, and remained in the possession of the family throughout most of the nineteenth century. Some of these Percy manuscripts were sold at Sotheby's in April 1884. The Miscellany appears as lot 272 in Sotheby's Sale Catalogue of 29 April:

272. Shenstone (W.). Collection of Poems transcribed and corrected from original MSS. Autograph MS. damaged at the edges by the fire in Northumberland House.

The manuscript is next heard of as in the possession of

J. G. Godwin, librarian to Lord Bute at Cardiff Castle. In the article on Richard Graves which W. P. Courtney contributed to the *D.N.B.* in 1890 it is referred to thus:

> Mr. Godwin possesses a manuscript collection of poems transcribed and corrected from original sources by Shenstone, which afterwards belonged to Bishop Percy. It includes numerous verses by Graves.

Godwin had an excellent collection of first editions of Graves, and the Shenstone Miscellany, presumably because it included unpublished poems by Graves, was part of it. Godwin died in 1896, and his Graves collection was acquired by Robert Drane of Cardiff. Sothebys sold Drane's library on 9 February 1916, and the next owner of the Graves collection was the firm of Maggs, who offered it to a New Zealand book-collector, Alexander H. Turnbull. At Turnbull's request the Miscellany was finely cased in green morocco, a special binding-case being made for the frail and charred Shenstone volume, with the title on the spine: 'Shenstone's M.S. Collections.' Turnbull's great collection of first editions and manuscripts was in 1918 bequeathed to the people of New Zealand, and the Alexander Turnbull Library, Wellington, is now controlled by the Department of Internal Affairs. Neither Turnbull nor the later library authorities identified the manuscript as the Miscellany which had been 'lost' for close on two centuries.

SHENSTONE AS AN EDITOR

The Miscellany is no mere commonplace book. The contents were gathered by Shenstone over a period of some four years and carefully chosen to illustrate his theory of poetry. First and most important are the verses of the Leasowes circle. They range from epigram to pastoral, but the emphasis is firmly laid on Shenstone's favourite qualities: simplicity, the pleasures of the country life, clear diction, and unaffected imagery. Lady Luxborough contributes a charming picture of country pleasures at Barrels, Mrs. Pixell naïve pastorals,

James Merrick a pastoral touched with the roguery of Gay, Shenstone's cousin, William Saunders, a pastoral ballad. Looking beyond the immediate circle of the Leasowes Shenstone gathered verse from others, an inscription for a Hermitage by Thomas Warton, and a ballad of country seats by the Earl of Bath. He also included verses which Somerville had written on Lady Luxborough's country hospitality and garden verses by Lady Mary Wortley Montague.

After pastorals Shenstone's next choice was songs, with a preference for easy skipping rhythms. Again the Leasowes circle was called in: Hylton, Shenstone's uncle William Penn, Whistler, Mrs. Pixell, and Shenstone's Edinburgh cousin Edward Cooke contribute their share. But the Leasowes group was not enough. He included several songs, published and unpublished, from earlier periods and from the operas of his day. So Richard Lovelace, Sir William Davenant, and the unknown author of a rousing song on the death of Queen Elizabeth find themselves included (without incongruity be it said) with lyrists writing for the music of Handel.

Of the Leasowes group the two most frequent contributors were Graves and Thomas Percy. Graves's poems are mainly epigrams, a form in which he excelled both openly and anonymously. Percy is represented by a group of poems, some of them never published. They range from an ode which contrives to lament the death of his patron while complimenting his successor on the improvements in his estate (a combination of pathos and landscape gardening that delighted both Grainger and Shenstone) to lyric translations from the Spanish and Chinese, and early lyrics to his wife.

Shenstone's direction of contemporary taste was in its quiet way influential. The school of minor poets whose work he drew on forms part of that eighteenth-century chorus of lesser singers whose themes and rhythms in a few years were to be recognized as the voice of romance itself. Nowhere is this forward glance of Shenstone seen more clearly than in a group of a dozen ballads which he included in the Miscellany.

Two were translated from the Spanish by Percy and submitted to Shenstone for his criticism. Three (*The Witch of
Wokey, Bagley-Wood*, and *Peytoe's Ghost*) are eighteenth-century
imitations. No fewer than seven are genuine ballads, five of
them chosen from Percy's famous Folio Manuscript: *Walsinghame, The Boy and the Mantle, Captain Carre, Gentle Herdsman*,
and *Old Sir Simon the King*.

Shenstone's share in the revival of interest in the ballad is
considerable. He was closely associated with the early stages
of the *Reliques*, an enthusiastic, if slow-moving, partner to the
more energetic Percy. The recent publication of Shenstone's
letters has revealed something of his contribution. As Percy's
voluminous letters and papers are brought into print (a task
long overdue) the part played by Shenstone will find fuller
recognition. B.M. Add. MS. 28221, a long correspondence
between Shenstone and Percy extending over the years 1757–
63,[1] shows that not only did Percy submit copies of many of
the ballads from the Folio Manuscript to Shenstone, but that
he was influenced by Shenstone in determining the choice of
pieces and the form in which they were printed. Percy's
unpublished diaries (B.M. Add. MSS. 32336, 32337) show
several records of his visits to the Leasowes. In October 1761,
for example, he spent a week there, conferring with Shenstone
on his Folio Manuscript and revising the ballads with his
help.[2] The unpublished correspondence of Percy and Sir
David Dalrymple, Lord Hailes (B.M. Add. MS. 32331), for
the years 1762 and 1763 contains further evidence of Shenstone's collaboration.[3]

Percy was an indefatigable worker. His three-volume *Reliques* appeared in 1765 and established his reputation. His
partner died in 1763 and the Miscellany remained unpublished. Perhaps it would have remained unpublished for
years even if Shenstone had lived. The publication of his col-

[1] Partially reprinted in Hans Hecht, *Thomas Percy and William Shenstone*
(Quellen und Forschungen, Hft. ciii), Strassburg, 1909.
[2] B.M. Add. 32336, fol. 34*b*.
[3] See the note to *Edom of Gordon*, p. 154.

lected works was deferred and deferred until in the end Dodsley put them out after the author's death. But the Miscellany note-book was filled by the beginning of 1763. It was neatly and carefully written, ready for the fine printing of 'neighbour Baskerville'—but it is idle to speculate. In the end Shenstone has had to wait for almost a couple of centuries.

PERCY AND THE MISCELLANY MANUSCRIPT

Percy handled all letters and manuscripts that came into his possession with detailed care, adding notes on allusions and short biographical memoranda, filling in gaps and occasionally heavily inking over names or passages he wished to delete. The process was continual. Many of the manuscripts in his library were worked over on different occasions, often years apart. Shenstone's Miscellany was no exception. Percy was familiar with many of the writers who had contributed, and could add personal details. He himself had provided Shenstone with unpublished material from various sources. Furthermore, when he examined the note-book he found copied there a group of his own poems. From time to time over a period of many years Percy annotated the Miscellany. One note (on Swift's *Dooms-day*) can be dated definitely as later than 1773. At least one note was added later than 1791. His own poems Percy edited with the utmost care, polishing the text, and even scratching out on occasion with a knife words or allusions which he preferred should not remain.

When Shenstone copied the poems into the Miscellany all but a few, as his 1759 title-page indicates, were unpublished. Had Baskerville printed the edition in 1763 or 1764 the Miscellany would have presented over fifty pieces for the first time. But even while Shenstone was copying the poems, a few of them were finding their way into print in the periodicals of the day: the *London Chronicle, Gentleman's Magazine, Annual Register,* and the rest. As the century proceeded poems in the Miscellany appeared in the collected works of the various poets. Even so a group of some thirty-five poems remains, by Percy, Lady Luxborough, Graves, and others, of which this edition seems to be the first publication. In the notes I have tried to trace contemporary publication, whether in periodical or in volume form. I have identified the authors (not all of them were known to Shenstone) and given brief biographical notes, particularly of the lesser-known figures. But the notes should not be regarded merely as explanatory of individual poems. They are meant in addition as a continuous commentary on Shenstone as he collected his material over four years and on Percy and Shenstone as a working partnership. By dovetailing the Miscellany to the correspondence of the two men we can almost look over their shoulders as they worked as critics and as editors.

In editing the Miscellany manuscript I have abandoned any attempt at a type-facsimile. The manuscript is so overwritten with variants by Shenstone and Percy and annotations (in the margins, on opposing pages, in the text, and in footnotes) by Percy that it would result in untidy pages in a printed form. The apparatus criticus gives detailed information of the treatment the manuscript received both while it was being revised from time to time by Shenstone, and during the long period when it was being continually annotated and expanded by his partner.

Shenstone's own pagination extends from p. 1 to p. 241. I have extended his pagination to include all pages after his p. 241, on which he had written no page-numbers. The volume may be described thus: Fly-leaf (to which original endpaper has been pasted)+i–iv+1–28, 33–88, 91–262+ original endpaper (pinned inside back cover). i–iv are pages of the original note-book left blank by Shenstone. His 'Title-page' is on p. 1 and his text begins on p. 3. All page references (except where otherwise indicated) in the apparatus criticus are to Shenstone's pagination.

Apart from a few instances referred to in the notes, the spelling and punctuation are as in the manuscript.

On the left side
of the sole building I can call my own
is consecrated
A MONUMENT
to the Memory of   5
the beloved and lamented
WILLIAM SHENSTONE:
It is formed something like an Urn
But of a substance so soft,
That all his Virtues   10
were with ease engraved on it;
Yet so tenacious,
They never can be erased:—
It is inscribed with affection and respect
for the gentle and elegant qualities   15
of which he was
the happy possessor;
And stamped with the deepest gratitude,
for the honour he had conferred
By his kind and condescending notice   20
on the
thereby dignified Owner.

The opposite Epitaph appear'd in the
London Chronicle Feb. 16, 1763 I conjecture it
to have been written by Miss Wheatley   25
T.P.

[p. i blank.]
1–22 [In Percy's 'printed' script.]
23–25 [Written by Percy in his normal cursive hand.]
[p. iv blank. Between p. iv and the following p. i the letter from Hylton referred to in the Introduction is bound in.]

A

COLLECTION

OF

POEMS

Transcrib'd & Corrected†

FROM ORIGINAL M.S.S.

BY

W. SHENSTONE

MDCCLIX

† Not universally corrected; some Pieces
having no occasion.

[Title-page laid out by W. S. in red and black printed script in imitation of a
printed title-page]

3

Ode to a Fairy

By MRS. GREVILLE

Molle meum levibus cor est violabile telis.

OFT have I teiz'd the gods in vain
  And pray'd till I've been weary
For once I'll seek my wish to gain
  Of Oberon the Fairy.

Sweet airy being! wanton sprite!   5
  Who livst in woods unseen
And oft by Cynthia's silver light
  Tripst gayly o'er the green

If e'er thy pitying heart was mov'd
  As antient stories tell   10
And for th' Athenian maid* that lov'd
  Thou soughtst a wonderous spell

Once more exert thy friendly pow'r
  Perhaps some herb or tree
Sov'reign as juice of western flowr*   15
  Conceals it's balms for Me.

I ask no kind return in Love   p. 4
  No charm to make me please
Far from my heart such gifts remove
  The heart that sighs for ease.   20

[Page 2 of the MS. is blank, apart from a note by W. S. repeating the Latin motto prefaced by the words: 'For a motto—to the Fairy Ode'. Pinned to p. 2 is a clipping (probably from the *London Magazine*, August 1761) with a slightly different text of the poem under the title 'A Prayer for Indifference'.]

Ode to a Fairy: W. S. had originally written 'perhaps' before 'By Mrs. Greville'. The word was then deleted.

15 *See Shakespeare's Midsummer's Night's Dream—Act.   Sc.   [Footnote, W. S.]

20 The: My q. [Queried variant by Percy, above line]

Nor ease nor peace that heart must know
  Which, like the needle true,
Turns at the touch of Joy or woe
  And turning trembles too.

Far as Distress the soul can wound   25
  Tis pain in each degree
And Bliss beyond a certain bound
  Expires in Agony.

Then take this treach'rous sense of mine
  Which dooms me still to smart   30
Which pleasure can to pain refine
  To pain new pangs impart.

Oh! haste to pour the lenient balm
  The languid nerve, to string
And, for my choice, serenely calm   35
  The Nymph Indifference bring.

p. 5 At Her approach, see hope & fear
  And expectation fly
And disappointment in the rear
  That blasts the promis'd Joy.   40

The tears that pity taught to flow
  Mine eyes shall then disown
This heart that throb'd for others woe
  Then hardly feel it's own

The wounds that now each moment bleed   45
  Shall then for ever close
And mild & tranquil days succeed
  To nights of sweet repose.

21 must: can [Percy, above line]
28 Expires in: Extends to [W. S. in margin]

6

O Fairy elf! but grant me this
 This one kind comfort send   50
And so may never-fading bliss
 Thy flowery paths attend.

So may the glow-worms glim'ring light
 Thy tiny footsteps lead
To some sweet regions of delight   55
 Unknown to vulgar tread.

And may thy acorn goblet fill'd   p. 6
 With heavn's ambrosial dew
From freshest fairest flowrs distill'd
 Pour forth it's stores for you   60

And what of Life remains for me
 I'll pass in sober ease
Half-pleas'd contented will I be
 Contented, half to please.

An Ode p. 7

By M iss W hite of Edgbaston*

W hither O whither flies the sleepy pow'r
Whose downy fetters bind the soul to rest?
Why, at this midnight, peace-inspiring hour,
My troubled mind with shapeless fears opprest?
Soft slumbers lenient aid I strive to gain   5
But ah I strive, I wish, I court in vain.

60 it's stores: fresh sweets [Percy, below line]
 * Daughter of the Revd. Mr. White former Rector of that Parish: after-
wards married to the Revd. ⟨   ⟩ Pixel ⟨   ⟩ [Footnote by Percy.
Badly charred]

Be still my stuttering heart; or tell me why
Soft-trickling steals away this melting tear
Why throbs my bosom with this painful sigh
For what from Fate has Innocence to fear   10
Resume thy wonted calm within my breast
And gently, gently beat thyself to rest.

Regard not Fancy; she with vagrant feet
Attends to lead thee far from peace astray
Or paint the shades where gentle shepherds meet   15
And blazon forth the Follies of the Day
While thou perhaps amid those shades will find
One gentle shepherd, to thy wish unkind.

p. 9

Verses on leaving * * * * in a
tempestuous night; March 22, 1758

By Mr. Percy

Deep howls the storm with chilling blast
   Fast falls the snow and rain
Down rush the floods with headlong haste
   And deluge all the plain.

Yet all in vain the tempest roars   5
   And whirls the drifted snow
In vain the torrents scorn the shores
   To Delia I must go.

9 throbs my bosom with this painful sigh [Supplied by Percy. Originally left blank]
   10 For: or [Original reading. Percy added the 'F']
   15 Or: To [Alteration by Percy above line]
   [p. 8 blank]
Title: The row of four asterisks is the final reading. W. S. had originally written 'A—'; Percy erased both the letter and the dash, and wrote four asterisks in the space. See Shenstone's index, p. 134.
   2 Fast: Quick [W.S.'s variant over original reading, deleted by Percy]
   8 Delia: [Original reading irrecoverably erased and 'Delia' inserted by Percy]

In vain the shades of evening fall
  And horrid dangers threat   10
What can the Lover's breast appall
  Or check his eager Feet?

The darksome vale he fearless tries
  And winds the pathless wood
High o'er the cliffs dread summit flies
  And rushes thro' the Flood   15

Love bids atchieve the hardy Deed   p. 10
  And act the wonderous part
He wings the foot with eagle-speed
  And lends the Lion-heart   20

Then led by thee, all-powerful boy
  I'll dare this hideous night.
Thy Dart shall guard me from annoy
  Thy torch, my Footsteps light.

The chearfull blaze, the social hour,   25
  The Friend—all plead in vain
Love calls—I brave each adverse pow'r
  Of Peril and of Pain.

For The Hermitage of John Ludford p. 11
Esq.

By MR. WARTON, Poetry-professor

BENEATH this stony roof reclin'd
I soothe to peace my pensive mind.
And while, to shade my lowly cave
Embow'ring trees their umbrage wave

10 horrid: [Written by Percy over an irrecoverable erasure]
24 Footsteps light: steps alight [W. S.'s variant in margin]
28 Peril: yearning [Partially erased original reading, amended by Percy.]

And while the maple dish is mine   5
The beechen cup unstain'd with wine
I scorn the gay licentious crowd
Nor heed the toys that paint the proud.

Within my limits lone and still
The blackbird sings in artless trill   10
Fast by my couch, cogenial guest
The wren has built her mossy nest
From social scenes, by nature wise
To lurk with Innocence she flies
Here hopes in safe repose to dwell   15
Nor aught suspects the silvan cell.

p. 12 At noon & eve I take my round
To mark how blows my flowery mound
And every budding primrose count
That trimly paints my blooming mount   20
Or o'er the sculpture's quaint and rude
Which deck my shady solitude
I teach, in many a wreath, to stray
Fantastick Ivy's gadding spray.

While such pure joys retirement wait   25
Who but would smile at guilty state
Who but would wish his peacefull lot
In calm oblivion's thoughtfull grott
Who but would cast his pomp away
To take my staff and mantle grey   30
And to the worlds tumultuous stage
Prefer the peacefull Hermitage.

11 cogenial [sic]

Peytoe's Ghost

By Mr. Jago

To Craven's health, and social Joy
   The festive night was kept
While mirth and patriot spirit flow'd
   And Dullness only, slept.

When from the jovial crowd I stole,   5
   And homeward shap'd my way;
And pass'd along by Chesterton,
   All at the close of day.

The skie with clouds was over-cast:
   An hollow tempest blowd   10
And rains & foaming cataracts
   Had delug'd all the road.

When thro' the dark & lonesome shade,
   Shone forth a sudden light;
And soon distinct an human Form   15
   Engag'd my wondering sight.

Onward it mov'd with graceful port
   And soon oertook my speed;
Then thrice I lifted up my hands
   And thrice I check'd my steed.   20

Who art thou, Passenger it cry'd
   From yonder mirth retir'd
That here pursu'st thy chearless way
   Benighted, and be-mir'd.

I am said I a country clerk   25
   A clerk of low degree
And yonder gay and gallant scene
   Suits not—a Curacy.

But I have seen such sights to-day
   As make my heart full glad.   30
Altho' it is but dark tis true
   And eke—my road is bad

p. 15 For I have seen Lords Knights & Squires
   Of great and high renown
To chuse a Knight for this fair shire   35
   All met at Warwick-town.

A wight of skill to ken our Laws,
   Of courage to defend;
Of worth to serve the publick cause,
   Before a private end.   40

And such they found, if right I guess—
   Of gentle blood he came;
Of morals firm, of manners mild,
   And Craven is his name.

Did half the *british* tribunes share   45
   Experienc'd Mordant's truth;
Another half like Craven boast
   A free unbiasst youth;

The sun, I trow, in all his race
   No happier state should find;   50
Nor Britons hope for aught in vain
   From warmth with prudence join'd

p. 16 Go on, my Country, favor'd soil
   Such patriots to produce!
Go on, my countrymen, he cry'd   55
   Such patriots still to chuse—

51 for: from [W. S.'s reading, amended by Percy]

12

This said, the placid Form retir'd
  Behind the veil of night;
Yet bade me, for my country's good,
  The solemn tale recite.   60

On the Death of Squire Christopher   p. 17
a remarkably fat Sportsman

Written, By M R. W I G S O N of University Coll., Oxon.

TIR'D with too long a chace, tho' stout,
For who can always hold it out
Old Christopher—and sure it grieves us
At last is lagg'd behind and leaves us
Has slowly taken natures road   5
And stumbled under his own load
As true an heart—denyt who dare
As drank his glass or carv'd his hare.
Then take the horn, and wind it o'er
The man who loved it so before.   10
Then let him sleep—& say no more.
Life breeds a throng; and Death must come
To thrust some out, to *make more room*.

In a blank leaf of the Siris   p. 19

By M R. G R A V E S.

IN Berkley's page whate'er he treats
  Appear both grace & ease.
Tar breaths forth aromatick sweets
  And metaphysicks please.

[p. 18 blank.]

13

Here batter'd rakes for taint or gout   5
    A sure balsamic find
Here Fops may read what Plato thought
    Of one eternal mind.

And who shall miracles deny
    If Berkley's pious care   10
Teach wits to own a Trinity
    And Beaux to relish Tar.

p. 20   A Parody of the speech of Jacques in
              Shakespear

                By Mr. Graves.

> *Rideri possit eo quod*
> *Rusticius tonso toga defluit, & male laxus*
> *In pede calceus haeret—at est bonus.*

Sir Plume—All the cloth are odd.
But all your Country parsons cursed odd-dogs.
They have their Foibles, & their Fopperies
And one remarks among them, sundry characters
To mention only seven—First the Curate   5
Humming & hawing to his drowsy herd
And then the pedant, with his horse-hair wig
And iv'ry headed cane ruling like Turk
Within his dusty school. Then the smart priest
Writing, extempore forsooth, a sonnet   10
Quaint to his mistress' shoe-string. Then the vicar
Full of fees customry with his burial gloves
One while with bridal cake, or sleepy tiff
Of cowslip wine, treating the sneering Squire
p. 21 Then jealous of his right & apt to quarrel   15
Claiming his paltry perishable tithes
Ev'n at the Lawyer's price. And then the rector

                    14

In sleek sur-cingle with good tithe-pig stuff'd
With eyes upswoln, & shining double Chin
Full of wise nods & orthodox distinctions 20
And so He gains respect. Proceed we next
Unto the old Incumbent at his gate
His Banyan with silver clasp, wrapt round,
His shrinking paunch, and his tam'd thundring voice
Now whistling like the wind his audience sleeps 25
And snores to th' lulling sound; perchance too dreams
E'er while there will be rain. Best scene of All
With which I end this reverend description
Is the welch parson with his noble Living
Sans shoes sans hose sans shirt sans—everything 30

Albeit I protest (says Owen Davis, a nettled welchman) I protest solemnly, & as I shall one day answer for the truth of what
I assert, that I never *did* see a welch parson without shoes &
stockings.

From the old M.S.S. Collection of Ballads p. 23

GENTLE herdsman, tell to me
    Of courtesy I thee pray
Unto the towne of Walsingham
    Which is the right & ready way.

Unto the towne of Walsingham 5
    The way is hard for to be gone
And very crooked are those paths
    For you to find out all alone.

[p. 22 blank.]

Were the Miles doubled thrice
    And the way never so ill   10
It were not enough for mine offence
    It is so grievous & so ill.

Thy years are young, thy face is faire
    Thy witts are weake thy thoughts are greene
Time hath not given thee leave as yet   15
    For to committ soe great a sinne

p. 24   Yes herdsman yes; soe wouldst thou say
    If thou knewest soe much as I
My wits & thoughts & all the rest
    Have well deserved for to dye.   20

I am not what I seem to be;
    My Clothes & sexe do differ farre;
I am a woman, woe is me
    Condemn'd to grief & irksome care.

†Ah friendly swain, be not surpriz'd   25
    Nor think my woefull story strange
The peerless wight for whom I grieve
    Has felt a farre more dismall change

25–36 [W. S. at some date after copying the poem inserted the following
footnote on p. 26:
    †The 3 following stanzas being very defective in the M.S. were supply'd
(unknown to me) in the following manner, by Mr. Percy.

            For my beloved & well beloved
                My wayward cruelty could kill
            And tho' I banisht him from sight
                Most dearly do I love him still

            He was the flower of noble wightes
                A youth more gentle neere colde be
            Of comely shape & miene he was
                And tenderlye he loved me.

            When thus I saw he loved me well
                I grew so proude his paine to see
            That I who did not know my self
                Thought scorne of such a swaine as he

            And grew &c:]

16

He was, to weet, a noble Impe
 Right blooming, beautifull & young   30
His manners too were gentle all
 As was the stocke from whence he sprung

Albeit he loved, & dearly loved
 He never could my pity move
Albeit I loved & dearly loved   35
 I could not bruike to tell my Love.

But grew so coy, & nice to please   p. 25
 As women's lookes are often so
He might not kisse my hand forsoothe
 Unless I willed him so to doe.   40

Thus being weary'd with delays
 To see I pitied not his greeffe,
He got him to a secret place
 And there he dy'd without releeffe

And for his sake these weedes I weare   45
 To sacrifice my tender age
And every day I'll beg my bread
 To undergo this Pilgrimage.

Thus every day, I fast & pray
 And ever will do 'till I dye   50
And get me to some secret place
 For soe did he, & so will I.

Now gentle heardsman ask no more
 But keep my secretts I thee pray
And to the towne of Walsingham   55
 Shew me the right & readye way.

37 But: And [Original reading, but amended by W. S. to link with his reconstruction of ll. 25–36.]

Now goe thy wayes; & God before!
For He must ever guide thee still
Turne downe that dale, the right-hand path
And soe faire Pilgrim, fare thee well!   60

Giles Collin; an old English Ballad

GILES COLLIN came home unto his mother,
 O Mother come bind my head
For before eight o'clock in the morning
 O Mother, I shall be dead.

And if that I should dye, dear Mother!   5
 As I foresee I shall
I will not be buried in the churchyard
 Save near Lady Annis's wall.

Lady Annis was sitting in her own bow'r
 And mending of her night-coif   10
When lo there appeared as fair a Corse
 As ever she saw in her life

She dropped her needle to the ground
 When she this corse did spy
She found her spirits sink apace   15
 And sigh'd—she knew not why.

What is it you bear you six tall Men
 Come lay it down & tell
We bear, we bear Giles Collins's corse
 Who lov'd Lady Annis so well.   20

3 in the morning: to-morrow [Variant added by W. S. in margin]

Lady Annis then viewd the young man's face
   She ey'd it oer & oer
Then fell she upon his clay-cold breast
   And word spake never no more.

Giles Collin's was buried in the west;   25
   Lady Annis's grave was east;
There sprung up a Lily from Giles Collins heart
   That reached Lady Annis's breast.

The butcherly Parson of the place,
   He cut this Lily in twain;   30
There never was known such a Parson before
   Nor will, such a Lily again.

[*No Title*]

Now this is the song the Brothers did sing   p. 33
   And sweetly well they play'd their part
Their Father He beat time the while
   And it tickled his majesty to the heart.

My Dog & I have learnt a trick;   5
To cure the maids when they are sick
When they are sick & like to dye
Then thither gangs my Dog & I.

My Landlady's maid, her name was Nell
A pretty young girl & I lov'd her well   10
I lov'd her well by reason why
Because she lov'd my Dog & I

[pp. 29, 30, 31, 32 have been torn out. Pages 29–30 had contained 'A ludicrous old ballad' and pp. 31–32 'George Riddle's oven; an old ballad'; cf. Shenstone's index, p. 253, where he forgot to delete the two entries. See notes.]

My mother she told me, & bade me note
That I should wear a thread bare coat
If I did follow tippling so   15
Good-ale would work mine overthrow.

p. 34
But if I should dye as I may perhap
My grave shall be under the good-ale tap
In folded arms there will I lie
Cheek by Jowl—my Dog and I.   20

p. 35

Bagley-Wood, A Parody

*occasion'd by Dr. Giles's panic apprehensions of
being robb'd there.*

GOD prosper long our 'Varsity
    Our Lives & purses all
A woefull robbery there did
    In Bagley-wood befall.

That fam'd Physician Doctor Giles   5
    A vow to God did make
In Abington's delightfull town
    Full many a Fee to take.

With pills & potions in his bags
    The Doctor took his way   10
The child may rue that is unborn
    The Physick of that day.

There having din'd he homeward look'd
    And left the staring mob
But first put up with special care   15
    His Fees within his Fobb.

When as to Bagley wood he came   p. 36
  His woefull Fears began
Samuel, my man, I'm much afraid,
  That rogues will us trepan.   20

O Master, you are in the right
  Five horsemen I espy.
Five daring rogues bedawb'd with dirt
  Let 's run before they're nigh.

The doctor in this dire distress   25
  No longer now demurrs
But to his steed, with might & main
  He claps his rusted spurs

His horse, tho' not for swiftness fam'd
  Then scour'd along the grove   30
Whoe'er had seen him would have swore
  The devil had him drove.

Now 'twas an honest country priest   p. 37
  That caus'd this dread alarm*
As peaceably he pac'd along   35
  Nor meant, nor dreamt of harm.

But when he saw the Doctors haste
  And heard his woefull cries
It seem'd no longer time to stay
  He too like lightning flies   40

As when the beaver men pursue
  He biteth off his stones
So this Divine behind him threw
  His purse to save his bones

28 He claps: Deep drives [Percy's variant below line]
33 Now 'twas: By chance [Original reading, amended by Percy]
33 *Strait Fellow of Merton [Percy's marginal note]
34 That caus'd this: Perceivd the [Original reading, amended by Percy]

Not so the wary Doctor Giles   45
    Tho frighted sore was He
His purse he kept—but his bea-ver
    Was caught up by a tree

This hat had many clouds of dust
    And many storms withstood   50
But then alas by cruel Fate
    'Twas lost in Bagley-wood.

p. 38 And when unto the town he came
    He met with Dame Wil-dare*;
And rais'd his hand to doff his hat   55
    And lo! it was not there

Then tidings to the warden† came
    A man piouse and gude
That Dr. Giles of his col-lidge
    Was slain in Bagley Wood   60

God rest his saoul, the warden saith
    Sith 'twill no better be
I trust I have in my collidge
    ‡Twenty as good as He

Yet shall not any robber say   65
    But I will vengeance take
And plague their hearts ten thousand ways
    For this poor doctor's sake

48 by: in [Marginal variant by W. S.]
54 *Mrs. Wilder Widow of the Revd. Mr. Wilder Author of 2 vols. of Sermons. 8vo. [Percy's marginal note]
56 it was not: no hat was [W. S.'s variant, above line]
57 †Dr. Wintle Warden of Merton a Scotchman. [Footnote by W. S. on p. 39, the words 'a Scotchman', being Percy's addition]
64 ‡The number of Fellows there; with whom the warden had disputes. [Footnote by W. S.]

Next day the reverend Priest did go
　　His purse for to bewail　　　　　　　　70
His cassock he bedew'd with tears
　　Which did at length avail

He found it humbled in the dirt　　　　　p. 39
　　And bore it fast away
And kissed it a thousand times　　　　　75
　　While it was clad with clay

God grant that Abington's fair town
　　May live in Health & peace
That Doctors and that highwaymen
　　In Bagley wood may cease.　　　　　80

An odd old Ballad　　　　　p. 41

The two first Lines chaunted; the four Last in Jigg-time.

I'LL tell ye good people all and I'll tell ye tru-ly
That ye never had more cause to lament and cry
　　O fie O fie O tell me why
　　Thou cruel cruel Death
Hast thou this Day kidnapped away　　　　5
　　Our good Queen Elizabeth.

II

Death might have taken other people that would have been
　　less misst
Than our good Queen Elizabeth who neither lov'd Pope nor
　　Priest.

80 N.B. Dr. *Giles*, a Physician Fellow of Merton College Oxon, was wont to
attend Abingdon Market; the foregoing Ballad was occasioned by a Panic, he
fell in coming home one evening, and by losing his hat in Bagley Wood. [Foot-
note by Percy]
　　[p. 40 blank]

23

Full 40 years she ruld this land
  Beholden unto No man   10
And govern'd the state of her own affairs
  Altho' she was but a woman.

III

p. 42 A woman said I—thats more than either you or I can tell
  So fair she was, & so chaste she was, that none knew her
    right well
A Monsieur he came out of Spain   15
  On purpose for to wooe her
But yet she liv'd & dy'd a maid
  Do all he could un-to her.

IV

She never did any thing in all her life that could in conscience
  prick her
Or suffer'd herself to be bully'd by him who calls himself
  Christ's vicar   20
Courageously she strove to fight
  Herself, beneath his banner
'Gainst Pope or Turk or King of Spain
  Or all that would trepann her.

V

p. 43 Had we Argus's eyes they'd all be to little for us to weep 25
  Since our good Queen Elizabeth, all at once, is fallen asleep.
Asleep said I—there may she lie
  Until the day of doom
And then she'll arise and piss out the Eyes
  Of the great old Pope of Rome.   30

A Solution

By ANTHONY WHISTLER ESQ.

ONE dark oenigma let me clear,
  Which has the world perplex'd
Tho I am no Philosopher
  And mine, a doubtfull text.

Why eager Man is soonest fir'd   5
  And soonest cloy'd in Love
While women, tho' at first retir'd,
  For ever constant prove

Is it not hence, by fancy wrought
  He for an angel sighs;   10
Till widely missing what he sought
  His baffled passion dies.

While They, with juster hopes inspir'd,
  Their utmost wish enjoy
And sharing all their breast requir'd   15
  Their Pleasures never cloy.

13 with juster hopes inspir'd: by no false hope betrayd [Percy's variant, above line]
14 wish: aim [Percy's variant, above line]
15 By disappointment unallay'd [Percy's variant, above line]
16 Their Pleasures: And find it [Percy's variant, above line]

Horace's 'donec gratus eram'

By the same

Horace

In those dear days when you confess'd my charms
  In those sweet moments while no happier boy
Around your bosom threw his wanton arms
  Lydia fond Lydia then was all my Joy
How smoothly pass'd the time of Love's gay spring   5
Your bard was happier than the Persian king

Lydia

In those dear days when I deserv'd your care
  In those soft hours when I engross'd your heart
While yet proud Cloe was not thought so fair
  Nor Lydia, slighted Fair endur'd the smart   10
Rais'd by your love to fame, to bliss divine
Not Ilias mighty name could match with mine

Horace

The Thracian Cloe now inflames my breast
  Sweet mistress of the song & vocal lyre
The Thracian Cloe is my Queen confest   15
  How soft the transports which her eyes inspire
For her I'd die, nor cruel death upbraid
If the kind Fates wou'd spare my darling Maid.

Lydia

The lovely Calais, now my only care
  Returns my passion with an equal flame   20
The lovely Calais, fresh as vernal Air
  Bright as a God & gentle as his frame

6 happier: richer [Percy's amendment, above line]
10 Fair: maid [Percy's amendment, above line]
14 vocal: warbling [Percy's amendment, above line]

For him I'd dye a thousand times with joy
If the blest Fates would spare the beauteous boy.

Horace

But say my Lydia say should Love return   25
  And with his brazen yoke our hearts unite
Should Thracian Cloe be repell'd with scorn
  And I my Lydias wonted smiles invite
Say, should my heart be open to her charms
Say would she once more fly into my arms   30

Lydia

Tho' he be fairer than the morning star
  The morning star bright harbinger of day
Tho you, than porous cork are lighter far
  Rough as the storms & changefull as the sea
To thy dear arms I'd resolutely fly   35
  With you I'd chuse to live; with you to dye.

Advice to a Preacher   p. 47

By DR. BYRON*

BRETHREN, this is to let you know
That I would have you to preach slow.
To give the words of a discourse
Their proper time, & life & force
To urge, what you think fit to say   5
In a sedate pathetic way
Grave & deliberate; as 'tis fit
To comment upon holy writ.

---

24 blest: kind [Percy's variant, below line]
26 brazen [Deleted by Percy] our hearts: our severd hearts [Percy's amendment above line]
 * Of Manchester, author of the song ⟨in⟩ The Spectator, My Time, O ye Muses [Percy's footnote]

Many a good sermon gives distaste
By being spoke in too much haste   10
Which, if it had been spoke with Leisure
Would have been listend to, with pleasure
And thus the Preacher often gains
His Labour only for his pains
As if you doubt it, may appear   15
From any Sunday in the year.

p. 48   For how indeed can one expect
The best discourse should take effect
Unless the Maker thinks it worth
Some care & pains to sett it forth   20
What does he think the pains he took
To write it fairly in a book
Will do the business—not a bit
It must be spoke, as well as writ

What is a sermon good or bad   25
If a man reads it, like a Lad
To hear some people when they preach
How they run o'er all parts of speech
And neither raise a word, nor sink
Our reverend Bishops one wou'd think   30
Had taken school-boys from the Rod
To make Embassadors of God.

p. 49   So perfect is the Christian scheme
He that from thence shall take his theme
And time, to have it understood   35
His sermon cannot but be good
If he will needs be preaching stuff
No time indeed is short enough
E'en let him read it like a Letter
The sooner it is done the better.   40

But for a man that has a head
Like yours or mine I'd like t'have said
That can upon occasion raise
A just remark, a proper phrase
For such an one to run along   45
Tumbling his accents o'er his tongue
Shews only that a man at once
May be a scholar—& a Dunce.

In point of sermons, tis confest   p. 50
Our English clergy make the best   50
But this appears, we must confess
Not from the pulpit, but the press
They manage with disjointed skill
The matter well, the manner ill
And, what seems paradox at first   55
They make the best, & preach—the worst

Would they but talk as well as write
Both excellencies would unite
The outward action being taught
To shew the strength of inward thought   60
How to do this, our short-hand school
Lays down this plain & general rule
Take time enough—all other graces
Will soon fill up their proper places.

A Song, by Miss White. Mutual Sympathy p. 51

AH who in all these happy plains
    With Collin can compare
A youth belov'd by all the swains
    Admir'd by all the Fair.

Title: [Last word slightly charred]

I think he 's free from artfull wiles   5
  For oft with tearfull eye
He fondly looks at me, & smiles
  He does—I know not why.

He press'd my hand—I gently sigh'd
  Yet hope he did not see   10
And then to speak he vainly try'd
  But gently sigh'd, like me.

Methinks this wary breast might know
  That men can feign a sigh
Yet when he 's nam'd it flutters so   15
  It does—I know not why.

Say gentle god, whose magic laws
  Controul both nymph & swain
Oh tell thy nymph the secret cause—
  The cause of Collin's pain   20

Say rather why this breast intreats
  The cause of Collin's woe
And why it flutters, why it beats—
  Alas!—too well I know.

P. 53 # Asteria in the Country To Calydore
in Town 1747–8

By the right hon. LADY LUXBOROUGH†

To you, my Friend,
From chearless hearths, & lonely grots I write,
Which once were scenes of Friendship & delight.
When zephyrs breath'd, where now the tempest roars;
And Linnets warbled, where the screech owl snores;   5

† Sister of Lord Bolingbroke [Percy's marginal note]

How pleas'd would you, at noontide, quit your rest
To hear the black-bird or to seek her nest
In grove obscure! where Phoebus rays to shun
I fondly view'd my sportive lambkins run
Or with Eliza, curious in each flow'r,   10
Cropt eglantine & rose to grace my bow'r
Dauntless we dar'd the thorny guard disdain
Well-knowing, pleasure *must* be bought with Pain
That season past, tho' driv'n from sun to fire
The genial blaze would wit & mirth inspire   15
While social friends around of converse mild
Asteria chear'd; her every care beguil'd.
Two nymphs, adorn'd with every pleasing art
To charm the fancy or engage the heart
Would with their pencil some fair Landskip trace   20 p. 54
Or stag, or hound—as just as in the chace
Our Somerville describes their pleasing race.
While courteous You, in matchless verse explain
The Deeds of mighty chiefs untimely slain.
Of Homer's heroes, nightly, let us hear   25
As Pope transmits 'em to the female ear
Or when you had reveald the Suitor's doom
Harangue of Cronstrom & of Berg-op-zoom
Till clocks unkind, & snoring slaves betray
How swift the social moment speeds away   30
Patty reluctant, Harriot more submiss
Part from Asteria with a friendly kiss
O! if so short an absence tedious prove
O think how must it their Asteria move
To find her favorite nymphs from Barels lost   35
For charms like theirs will soon be Londons boast
And who can leave the town, when once a toast
Three sisters more will grace your smoaky town
For matron-like my lov'd Johannah's gone
That parent-bird, with five fair chirpers blest,   40 p. 55
To warm, to skreen them in her downy breast.

To these succeeded at Asteria's board
What seldom schools or colleges afford
A parish-priest; nor fop, nor unpolite
Tho' comely yet not vain; tho' gay not light;   45
Tho' young yet learn'd; no pedant, nor no clown
Of morals good—as well becomes the gown.
   Next came with friendly zeal, as well you know
Thro' trackless roads, oer mountains pild with snow
Our own Salopian bard*; the muse's friend   50
Taught high to soar; yet deigning here descend
To lowly chat, & to as lowly fare
At whist to play, or loll in elbow chair.
Tho' uninspiring such amusements seem
Thro these we saw his piercing genius beam   55
He sung, yet undeserving was his theme
In softest verse Asteria's praise he sung
For never left the muse his lyre unstrung
The sister arts alike attend his call
And fancy joins, & nature smiles on all   60
p. 56 While gratefull he to nature, of her charms
Enamor'd sings; nor heeds the fate of arms
If peace at Aix, or war in zealand reign
Who lose their ground, or who their ground maintain.
But with unerring taste, the dame his guide,   65
Her steps to trace his pleasure & his pride
He forms elysian shades in his retreat
His house, like good Laertes rural seat
Farm-like adorn'd, but elegantly neat
The charms, the sweet environs of his place   70
No phrase uncouth to men gallic race
Let Thomson tell; or Virgil's awfull shade
If e'er it stalk along your pensive glade
From whence, mid groves of poplar, it may view
Just honors paid, where every praise is due   75
There plaintive Naids leave their spatious bed

50 *Mr. Shenstone [Percy's marginal note]

32

And tears incessant round his column shed
While peacefull Dryads, listning to the sound
Protect from busy fiends the sacred ground
Nature herself in Baice's blissfull clime   80 p. 57
Preserves his tomb from all-devouring time
With myrtle bands, & ivy wreaths imbrowns
With ever beauteous bay spontaneous crowns
His dust rever'd—Our bard records his fame
In humble offerings to his deathless name   85
And shews, whene'er he tunes the votive lyre
How much his great Idea can inspire
Could I, like Him, attune my artless reed
I'd sing like Shenstone; sing each flowery mead
Each fertile field enrich'd with flocks or grain   90
Each spiral grove—above my rustic strain
Where the delighted eye from lawns to hills
Unweary'd wanders o'er meandering rills
Where artfull toils to nature homage pay
Assist but never check her lawfull sway   95
    Return'd to these, the tiremaids of his woods
Or gone to scoop new windings for his floods
The Bard to us is lost—& so are you
O Calydore! sincere amongst the Few
Who to that noblest praise a right may claim   100 p. 58
From real acts of Friendship, not the Name.
The Chaplain's visit here I'd gladly place
But apparition-like he shew'd his Face
And yielding up to cares the social flame
Surpriz'd us when he went, & when he came.   105
    Great change & dire at poor Asteria's cott
Silence & solitude her hapless Lot!
Unjoyous days, & evenings full of thought
Yet happy still; & still with pleasure fraught
Were present bliss reflection on the past   110
Her hoarded treasure then might ages last

89 like Shenstone [Written by Percy above a row of self-effacing ×'s by W. S.]

But much I fear Regret were too reviv'd—
For sublunary joys are all short-liv'd.
    May yours be long—not trivial as these rhimes
Less tunefull than some squirrels tiresom chimes   115
Yet not so pleas'd with jingle as to think
Like Prior's squirrel that I rise, I sink
Alas from Prose like verse to verse like prose
Like as the Painter's Lion to his rose.

p. 59   Why then, you cry, on me bestow your trash?   120
A rhimeing Princess cuts a tinsel Flash.
Hold courteous Heroe! tho' unskill'd in Art
Alike my tongue, my pen, & friendly heart
And rude my Lays—receive at least my pray'r,
May happiness unchecquer'd be your share.   125

p. 60   A Receipt for a modern Urn

                    By PARSON ALLEN; Extempore

FORTY five mottos full of odd Hints
Nicely engrav'd on forty five Plinths
An heart-melting epitaph scrawld on the urn
With alas! & alack! he will never return
Forty five Cherubims weeping a show'r   5
The three fatal sisters—in a dark bow'r
Pan & his shepherds dolefully piping
And the nymphs—dolefully—*their* faces wiping
Each emblematical shrub that e'er grew
Twisted in wreaths with sad Cypress & yew   10
With a pedestal bold, as the mountainous pillar
That lately was built by Mr. Millar.

115 some [Scored out in MS.]
125 The words courteous, unjoyous, Heroe, Princess, used frequently in the
circle of acquaintance to which this Poem bears allusion. [Footnote by W. S.
to whole poem]
12 Mr. Millar [Percy's amendment. W. S. had written a row of asterisks]

34

Song, by Mr. Somerville to Lady Luxborough

p. 61

How do busy Fools employ
Ages, barren of all joy?
Pow'r & sordid gain pursuing
Proud, triumphant in undoing
At Asteria's board refin'd   5
Beauty, wit & science join'd
Bless our ears, & charm our eyes
Who so happy, who so wise?

Still improving, ever gay
Can we better spend the day   10
In so mild, so pure a Light
Can we ever think it night
Tyrant sleep, intruding pow'r
Claim not thou this blissfull hour
Whilst we rival those above;   15
Thus to learn, & thus to love!

Under M. Queen of Scots, The Face resembling Miss Ebourne

p. 62

By MR. BINNEL

HAPPY the Few, to whom fair Queen, 'tis giv'n
Like you to share the rosy bloom of heav'n
Happier if they with no foul vice deface
Like you their rising charms their native grace
When the fair frame as fair a mind contains   5
The union bends to earth the suppliant swains

35

Without constraint they chearfull homage pay
While virtue teaches beauty how to sway
'Tis thus Matilda graces Mary's mien
She therefore shines *my* saint—she reigns my Queen. 10

p. 63

Mr. Jago to Miss Fairfax on * * *

By MR. JAGO

WHEN Nature joins a beauteous Face
With shape & air & life & grace
To every imperfection blind
I pardon Frailties of the mind.
When wit with lively Lustre shines   5
And decks her converse or her lines
My ravish'd heart Lauretta warms
And well can spare external charms.
Good-nature with success may sue
The void of wit, & beauty too.   10
When gen'rous thoughts a breast inspire
I wish it's wealth, & honours higher
When Beauty, Wit, & Kindness meet⎫
With large Demesnes, & soul as great⎬
An earthly Deity's compleat.   ⎭   15
But should I see a sordid mind
With affluence & ill-nature joind

p. 66

And Pride, without a grain of sense
And, without beauty, Insolence
The Creature, with comtempt I'd view,   20
And sure 'tis like Miss—you know who.

18–21 [W. S. had turned over two leaves of his note-book and these four
lines are at the head of p. 66. He adds a footnote at the end of p. 63, 'Vid.
conclusion Page 66.' Percy added a further signpost at the head of p. 66, 'See
begin. P. 63.', thus correcting a further error by W. S. who had written at the
head of p. 68, 'See the beginning in pag. 63']

Written Oct: 1761

p. 64

By MR. GRAVES

THREE Georges now, for Britain's welfare born,
To latest times her annals shall adorn
The First, tho' view'd with Party's envious eyes
Contending Faction's own—was good & wise
Thro a long reign tho' still by parties mov'd   5
The *second* George we stile the well-belov'd
Behold a youth ascends the British throne
Whom *every* royal virtue calls his own
Proceed young Prince! a patriot King compleat
And George the third henceforth be GEORGE the
    GREAT.   10

Sept. 22, 1761

By the same

An abridgment of the University Verses to the Queen. 1761

JUNO 's a brimstone—Dian's self's an Harlot
Matchd with the chaste, the mild, the royal Charlotte.

On Mr. Pitt's return to Bath, after his Resignation 1761

p. 65

By MR. GRAVES

BRITANNIA long her wretched Fate had mourn'd
By Factions rent, at home; by Europe scorn'd.
To guide her tottering barque, a Pilot fit
She sought with anxious eye; & fix'd on Pitt.

2 her: our [W. S.'s marginal variant]
5 long reign tho' still by parties mov'd [Percy's addition. W. S. had left the space blank]

Pitt left these Founts of health, & active rose. 5
Revivd her credit & subdued her Foes
Nay more—He bade ev'n civil discord cease,
And saw embittered Factions meet in peace
Then quits the Helm—without a title, great;
And seeks once more at Bath a calm retreat 10
Great Cincinnatus thus, at Rome's request,
Left his lone Farm, assum'd the purple vest,
Brandish'd the sword; by patriot zeal inspir'd
Just sav'd his country—triumph'd—& retir'd.

p. 66 On Mr. Pitt's Resignation. 1761

WHEN first portentous it was known,
That George had jostled from his Crown
    The brightest diamond there;
The Omen-mongers, one & all,
Foretell some mischief must befall; 5
    Some loss, beyond compare.

Some fear this Gem is Hanover;
While others wish to God it were;
    Each strives the nail to hit;
One guesses that; another, this; 10
All mighty wise, yet all amiss,
    For None e'er thought of Pitt.

6 Revivd: Retrievd [Variant by W. S., above line]
10 Bath: Hayes [Variant by W. S., above line]
12 purple: imperial [Variant by W. S., above line]

In the scotch Manner, by

The REVRD. MR. WILL. SAUNDERS

THE Lass of the west was witty & free;
Her Looks gay & winning, her eyne full o' glee,
And many a young Damon had Nancy in view,
But none lov'd like Willy; like Willy so true.

In a cool poplar shade, near a slow-running stream, 5
The shepherd thus warbled, & Love was his theme:
While I strive to be free, I am limed all o'er;
And the more that I struggle, am tangled the more.

Over hills & high mountains, full far have I been;
Fine assemblies, in fair towns, full oft have I seen; 10
By the banks of rough Severn, by smooth-gliding Thame,
Thro' gay London Damsels, right heart-free I came!

But, unweeting Loon, that westway must roam!
Whose heart had been free, had I bided at home!
Now with Love o' fair Nancy my heart runneth o'er, 15
And the more that I strive—I am tangled the more.

When lonely I wander, my flock goes astray;
While I fondly sit wishing swift time flies away;
With swift-flying time, all nature is borne,
The Lasses all lovely, the Lads all love-lorn! 20

The Jasmin, the rose, & the carnation—dye
And my brighter Nancy must withering lie:
In my bosom I'd bear thee thro' Life my sweet Flow'r;
And shelter thee safe from the wind & show'r.

Stella

A pastoral monody, on the Death of Miss Yelverton,* a relation to Ld.
Sussex (obt. Jan: 30th, 1754, Aetatis 19)

By the R EVRD. M R. H UCKELL

STRETCH'D in a melancholy shade
Long steep'd in tears bewaild a joyless swain.
  In silent sorrow for the peerless Maid:
  At length he snatch'd the Lyre
And chang'd the strings to such a plaintive strain   5
  As art-neglecting grief is wont inspire.
And come he cry'd—come hither ev'ry muse
For never did ye yet your aid refuse
  Invok'd in Stella's everpleasing name
Ah no! you lov'd her & with pleasing care   10
Wou'd weave her chaplets, or her seat prepare
  Within the temple of immortal Fame
But hard necessity now bids me ask
Your sad assistance in the bitterest task.

  Her vital lamp is quench'd by death   15
  And with her parting breath
Young hope, & rosy pleasure took their flight
And tearfull grief extinguish'd ev'ry light.

Alas where now are all those flow'ry lays
Which late ye deckt with Fancy's choicest store   20
And fondly fashion'd to the fair one's praise
Her boundless virtue's all unequal meed.
Go hang them now around her sable herse
And bid the Vain, & bid th' ambitious read
  The monitory verse.   25
For sure if beauty or if worth could save
She ne'er had sunk into the silent grave.

---

* Only Daughter of the Honble. Henry Yelverton, Uncle to the present
Earl of Sussex. [Percy's footnote]
  2 bewaild: bewaid [MS. reading]

Late in those eyes whose sweetly temperd ray
Shone like the kindest stars propitious Light
Expressive wit, & modest sense were seen   30 p. 71
And every swain who trod the daisy'd green
Vow'd the fresh rose could not such charms display
As those pale cheeks, whose easy smiles express'd
The noble freedom of her blameless breast
And vainly, vanquisht Philomela strove   35
    If thro' th' attentive grove
The gracefull Stella pour'd her sweeter song
Diffus'd from those blest Lips which never knew
To speak a language various from the heart
Those Lips unskill'd in the mysterious art   40
Of less'ning merit, or encreasing wrong
Whence the chill breath of slander never flew
But the mild voice of universal love.
Haste to the woods, ye gratefull shepherds go,
Search the pied mead, or climb the moss-clad hill   45
And search the marge of each lamenting rill   p. 72
For every bud that sips the morning dew
Of fragrant breath, or lovely hue
And hither quick your bloomy burthen bring
And strew the sweets upon her virgin bier   50
    Alas ye seek in vain!
For see the gloomy sign of gen'ral woe
All unadorn'd proceeds the lifeless year
And slights th' endearments of the wanton spring
    While on the dreary ground   55
He thinly throws the drooping snow-drops round
    Descriptive of that early hour
When, e'er the vernal days of Life were fled
Fate's icy Fingers pluck'd this lovely flow'r

But what avails it with incessant sighs   60
    To pierce the senseless Air
Or drink so deep the bitter cup of Care

p. 73 She reigns in bliss above the spangled skies
It not avails—but where can we obtain
The soft Lethe'an draught, or where evade 65
Fond memory that still before our eyes
Brings the fair picture of the gracefull maid
And feeds the fancy with the pleasing pain.
Oft as around my wandering eyes I throw
Charm'd with the rural scene & pleas'd survey 70
The flow'r-invested lawns or mark how flow
The babling brooks along their rushy beds
Or how the high hills heave their purple heads
Or visit with my view the cottage low
The balmy breathing herds, the crowded fold 75
And nature's sweet diversity behold
Alas for her, whose happy hand so well
Cou'd spread the valley or the mountain swell
With beauties all the growing scene invest
And rival busy nature's fair design 80
Of nature's various works herself the best—
p. 74 Nor can the warbling reed afford relief
My simple Ditties chearless I rehearse
Lamenting that the gentlest muse is fled
The fairest subject of the shepherd's verse 85
And yet to fly the close pursuit of grief
In vain I mingle with the rural Throng
Brisk Corin, late so full of wanton wiles
And every laugh creating Jest
In friendly sorrow strikes his libral breast 90
And good Damoetas too, the carefull swain
Who skillfull can detect the secret pow'r
Of every dew-fed herb, or potent Flow'r
Or with unerring Fingers can pursue
Enchanting harmony's mysterious clue 95
That leads the soul in rapture to the skies
Or well can weave the fancy'd Carol sweet
Now flings upon the ground his pensive eyes

42

And wants the skill to cure his bosom's pain
And ev'ry youth forbears the jocund song   100 p. 75
The frolick revel & the sprightly dance
And every nymph bewails the sad mischance.

O say ye virtues! had not ye the Pow'r
To gain a respite for your favrite Maid
For you, the spotless virgin ne'er forsook   105
Thou smiling Patience with your sister veild
Fair Piety that shuns suspicious Art
And thou bright charity with hands conceald
Could ye not longer warm that gen'rous heart
And couldst not Thou, young Innocence awhile   110
Charm the grim tyrant with thy heavenly smile
Nor thou, sweet modesty, with Cherub Look
Or thou prevail O blest with endless youth
Firm gratitude—or thou resistless truth
Spread thy white robe before the fatal Dart   115
Alas 'twas you our early hopes betrayd
    And clos'd so soon her Date
So near ye plac'd her to the blissfull gate   p. 76
Bore her so high toward her native heav'n
Refin'd & loosend from inferior tyes   120
That when she heard the first short summons given
Her soul took wing & sought it's kindred skies
    The swain his sorrows selfish all & vain
Thus rudely fitted to his Doric lays
While she blest angel with that heavenly choir   125
Who wrapt in endless pleasure never hear
The voice of grief, or see the flowing tear
Attunes her new cœlestial Lyre
And ravish'd listens to the blissfull strain
Of deathless Joys & everlasting Praise.   130

43

An Epitaph from Cheltenham Church-yard On an Infant

p. 77

To keep me harmless from ensuing crimes
Nature, soft nurse put me to bed betimes.

Another, on Miss Forder

SOFT sleep thy dust, & wait th' almightys will,
Then rise unchang'd, & be an Angel still!

Horace. Book II. Ode the 12th

p. 78

Addrest to Lord X   By—BAGOT Esq.†

OF battles won, & Kings in chains
   Let other Poets sing
To nobler themes in nobler strains
   Sublimely sweep the string.

Too harsh are those for Me—my youth   5
   A gentler goddess warms
To sing of Innocence & Truth
   To sing Licinias charms

Licinia, chearfull easy gay   10
   Amid the virgin-throng
Who charms us in each festive play,
   The Jest, the Dance, the song

O say what hearts thy beauty fires
   When in the Dance you move
When heavenly gracefulness inspires   15
   The tenderness of Love.

† Student of Xt. Church. Written before he left school. [Footnote by W. S.]

Wou'd you, my Lord, for all the stores p. 79
   That wave on Phrygia's plain
Would you for all the pretious ores
   Arabian mines contain   20

For these for all that's rich & rare
   Twixt Ganges & the Rhine
Of bright Licinia's glossy hair
   One single braid resign.

While on her neck it loosely plays   25
   Her neck tow'rd you reclin'd
While every Look & Gesture says
   She's going to be kind.

Now glowing with disorder'd charms
   Majestically coy   30
Now springing eager to your arms
   To meet the promis'd joy.

An Impromptu; to Seignior Francisco: p. 80

By MR. HYLTON of Coventry Jan: 19, 1729

SAY happy Bard, Apollo's eldest son,
   Say whence can it ensure,
That late last night, with Punch replete,
   I dreamt so much of *you*?

Your hand with generous care supply'd   5
The mighty goblet's rowling tide;
   With mystic trophies grac'd:
The waxen taper brightly shone,
   With all in order plac'd.

23 Of: From [Original reading, corrected by W. S.]

45

O Joy! O rapture to my soul! 10
  I saw the large capacious bowl,
  Full flowing with delight!
Francisco smil'd, & with a Nod
Said Grace, for once, & blessed his God
  For such a glorious sight. 15

p. 81 Now in Allegro we drink briskly on,
And laugh & drink, & drink to laugh again,
    Inspir'd with nectar; gayly we attend
      The pleasing health, that dances round
    To this man's Lass, to that man's Friend; 20
      And wit & Mirth abound:
Mirth without madness, wit with wisdom join'd,
At once to profit, & to please the mind.

But Lo! the ebbing bowl declares
  A Period to our joy; 25
True emblem of Mortality:
When we, with quantum suffict of Life
    And with a thankfull heart,
      Shake honest hands
      And gravely slow 30
All in Adagio part!

p. 82 O Frank! if Dreams this pleasure give,
  What shall we not partake,
When all these dreams are verify'd,
  To Fancies full awake? 35

35 Fancies: Senses [Percy's variant in margin]

To the Memory of R. West of Pope's in Hertfordshire, i June 1742.

London Evning P.

WHILE surfeited with Life each hoary Knave
Grows *here* immortal & eludes the grave
Thy virtues prematurely met their Fate
Crampt in the Limits of too short a date
Thy mind, not exercis'd so oft in vain   5
In health was gentle, & compos'd in pain
Successive trial still refin'd thy soul
And plastic Patience perfected the whole
A friendly aspect, not suborn'd by art
And eye which look'd the meaning of the heart   10
A tongue with simple truth & Freedom fraught
The faithfull Index of thy honest Thought
Thy pen disdain'd to seek the servile ways
Of partial censure or more partial praise
Thro every tongue it flow'd, with nervous ease   15
With sense to polish, or with wit to please
No lurking venom from thy pencil fell
Thine was the kindest satyr—living well
The vain, the loose, the base might wish to see
In what thou wert, what they themselves should be. 20
Let me not charge on Providence a crime
Who snatch'd thee blooming to a better clime
To raise those virtues in an higher sphere
Virtues, which only could have starv'd thee here.

47

Epigram 1752

Aт the Squire's long board, in the days of Queen Bess
Sate the Fool to make sport, & the chaplain to bless.
But frugal Sir Flint has contracted the Rule
And Bibo's to serve both for Chaplain—and Fool.†

Percy

p. 85

Epigrams

My Lord complains that Pope stark mad with gardens
Has lopp'd three trees, the value of—three Farthings
But he's my Neighbor quoth the Peer polite
And if he'll visit me—I'll wave my right—
What, on compulsion! & against my will   5
A Peer's acquaintance—Let him file his *Bill*.

Pope

Epigram on the Proclamation of War
(Mr. Graves)

Tнe Sov'reign, at St. James's gate
Unsheath'd the mystic sword of state

See †Cambden now proclaims defiance;
Let Europe tremble at th' Alliance.

1752: [Date added by Percy]
3 contracted [Percy's amendment over an erasure. He adds a footnote: 'the original reading']
4 †A Parody of Pope's Epigram on Colly Cibber [Percy's footnote]
† A village in Glostershire. [Footnote by W. S.]

Song†

By WILLIAM PENN of Harborough, Esq:

How can you, my Dear
In Frowns still appear
 That freeze the fond heart of your Lover?
When Kindness would warm
And brighten each charm;   5
 And your smiles wou'd your beauty discover.

Then banish my Care
And repell my Despair;
 Lest, at length, you have cause to repent it:
Lest, at length, you shou'd cry,   10
When expiring I lie,
 'His Death I might have prevented'.

Pembroke the simple to XtChurch the Ample (Mr. Graves)

TRUCE with thy sneers, thou proud insulting College!
Altho' *unknown*, we may be Men of Knowledge.

Mammas atque Tatas habet Afra etc.

By the Same

THO Pappa, & Mamma, my dear,
 So prettily you call;
Yet you, methinks, your *self*, appear
 The grand-Mamma, of *all*.

† Preserv'd, as the only relique of my uncle's Poetry. [Footnote by W. S.]
 Mammas atque Tatas l. 4. The grand-Mamma of all: or Great Grandmother
of all [W. S.'s variant below line]

An Oeconomical reflection,

by the same

ALL mortal things are frail & go to pot;
What wonder then if mortal Trowsers rott?
My velvet, torn, I shone in mimick Shagg,
Those soon grew rusty, & began to flagg.
Buck'skin was greasy; Serge-de-nim was queer,   5
Fustian was glossy—*this* I cou'd not bear.
Quoth I, Sir Pricklouse: shall we try a Rugg;
Aye Sir, says he, that sure will hold a Jugg
Ah no! the rugg decay'd like all the past;
Ev'n Ever-lasting, would not ever last.   10
At length, judge how I fix'd it; why in troth
With projects tir'd, I stuck to common Cloth.

p. 88

p. 91

Yesterday

*being the Counterpart of To-morrow published in Dodsley's
Poems vol: 4 p. 255.*

By DR. COTTON, Physician at St. Albans

WELL, yesterday is past, & cannot be
Recall'd—what did we yesterday, Horatio?
Did we or good or bad? Let us reflect—
It must not be forgot; for in the book
Of Heav'n tis minuted—did we transgress?   5
Doubtless we did—but Heav'n is mercifull—
Yet Let us not abuse Heavn's mercy: our duty
Is true repentance—what is repentance askst thou,
To mourn the Follies past repent the Future—
Prevent the future! mind; for Cries & tears   10

An Oeconomical Reflection ll. 5, 6. [W. S. indicates that these lines should be
transposed]
   [pp. 89, 90 torn out]

50

Alone are vain—yet who can think we have
Incens'd the universal sovereign
Without a Flood of Tears? at every Fault
Of Mine, whenever I remember it
My heart weeps blood, then let us in to penitence   15
But sure we have not always sin'd—not always
Some good we do—I yesterday reliev'd
A censur'd Friend—his Crime was Poverty
And, with my gold, I gave him reformation
In the worlds eye, & reconcil'd it to him   20 p. 92
And thou, Horatio!—'twas a noble Act
Didst save a beauteous maid from violation
O how her Virtue struggled with her want
That most inhuman Tyrant!—O want!
Thy whips cut deep, & force the wise & good   25
Oft to obey thee, in deeds their souls abhor.
'My poverty, but not my Will consents'
Sings Fancy's sweetest Child accursing want,
Had not thy powerfull hand prevented it
Had surely forc'd her   30
Let us persist in actions such as These:
So shall to-morrow smiling yield us Comfort;
And every day the same—till death the Friend
The truest Friend to Innocence & Virtue
Shall come benign to usher to the Court   35
Of the celestial Prince, whose plaudit waits us,
And all the Host of Heav'n, shall shout us 'Welcome.'

From Mr. Percy

Un Soneto de Cervantes   p. 94

MARINERO soi d'amor
   Y en su pielago profundo
Navigo sin esperanza
   De llegar a puerto alguno.

[p. 93 blank]

51

Siguendo voi a una estrella   5
  Que desde lexos discubro
Mas bella y mas resplandeciente
  Que quantos vio Palinuro.

Yo no se adonde me guia
  Y assi navego confuso   10
El alma a mirarla attenta
  Cuydadoso y con descuydo.

Recatos impertinentes
  Honestad contra el uso,
Son las nueves que me l'encubran   15
  Quando mas verla procuro.

p. 96

O Clara* y luciente estrella!
  En cuya lumbre m'appuro
Al punto que me t'encubras
  Sera de mi' muerte el punto   20

p. 95

A celebrated sonnet, from the Spanish of Cervantes

THRO' Love's profound & stormy main
  An hapless mariner I sail
Nor hopes my weary bark to gain
  Or welcome port or friendly gale.

Led by a star* my course I steer   5
  Ah too remotely shine it's rays
A lovelier star did neer appear
  To faithfull Pilot's watchfull gaze

17 *El nombre de la Dama. [Footnote copied by W. S. from his original]
5 *Alluding to her Name *Stella* [Percy's footnote]

Regardless wheresoe'er it lead
    With crowded sail I follow on   10
Nor lurking Rocks, nor shallows heed
    Attentive to it's rays alone.

Yet oft the Clouds of cruel slight
    Reserve & Coldness interpose
And hide them from my longing sight   15
    At random then my vessel goes.

O peerless star, whose ray divine   p. 97
    Preserves me still, in tempests tost:
Shouldst thou no longer on me shine
    I sink for ever, wreck'd & lost!   20

              By Mr. Percy

The Disappointment *
                                  p. 99

MIRA the Toast of half our sex
Whose blooming cheeks dame Venus decks
    With Roses & with Lilies
Who looks a goddess, moves a Queen
And if she sing, how clearly seen   5
    The muse's tunefull skill is.

Mira, as late I chanc'd to greet
With looks how affable and sweet
    Return'd the charming creature!
To-day I ran to meet the Fair   10
But Lo! Scorn triumph'd in her Air
    And glow'd in every feature.

16 my [Written by Percy over an erasure]
*Written about 1753 [Percy's note on p. 98, which is otherwise blank]·
5 if she sing, how clearly: whose note so clearly [Percy's variant, above line]
7 as: whom [W. S.'s reading, amended by Percy]
9 Return'd [written in by Percy over an erasure]

To learn whence all this sudden Pride
To Venus I my prayrs applied
　　And brib'd her with a sonnet　　　　　15
Ah Dupe! reply'd the laughing Queen
That marks yon azure skie, serene
　　And then depends upon it.

p. 100
Know when she did her smiles bestow
The nymph had newly left her beau　　20
　　But now the occasion varies
Think not from her a smile can fall
Who shone last night at Cynthio's ball
　　'Mongst lords and lady-Maries

Go change your notes ye witling train　　25
No more the constant sex profane
　　By likening, to the seas 'em:
They're formed you see by different Laws
Since Fortune's chilling tempest thaws
　　And warmest sun-shines freeze 'em.　　30

　　　　　　　　　by Mr. Percy.

p. 101

Pluto and Proserpine

from the French of Mons: de la Motte

By Mr. Merrick

How Pluto once thro Inna straying
O'er took young Proserpine a-maying
And how the nymph of lovely feature
Was frighted at the ugly Creature

19–24 [This stanza was not copied by W. S.　　Percy at the top of p. 100
adds a note: 'The Stanza below to come in here'. Half-way down the page
he notes: 'omitted above', and then transcribes the text of the omitted stanza]
28 different: other [W. S.'s reading, amended by Percy]
31 'By' [Inserted by Percy over an erasure, possibly: 'from']

How, as he bore her off, by dozens   5
She call'd her sisters aunts & Cousins
All this & more who doubts may look
And read it in a printed book.
   When Ceres the Disaster knew
In frantick mood away she threw   10
Her wheaten garland & her head-dress
And ran to Jove to seek for redress
Vex'd to the heart at what was done
And griev'd to see her so take on
Jove thus reply'd—Thou knowst, my Child   15
These younger brothers are so wild
Tis vain to try by threats or favor   p. 102
To bring the Lads to good behaviour
However—to preserve our Quiets
(Because I hate domestic riots)   20
Here, Mercury, a message bear
To Pluto; tell him, one half year
The Damsel shall be His; but t'other
I bid him yield her to her Mother.
I know the rogue this curb will bear ill   25
But let him murmur at his peril.
He said; & swift as Carrier-pigeon
Young Hermes sought the nether region
The message rous'd the monarch's spirit
See how these upstarts domineer it   30
Have I oppos'd this Lord of yours
Or interfer'd in his amours
That he presumes with lawless seizure
Thus to abridge me of my Pleasure.
Go tell him—Hold cries young Mercurius   35 p. 103
Uncle of mine—be not so furious
Thou knowest, it boots not to debate
Jove wills—& what he wills is Fate
He said—full well the Monarch knew
That what the stripling said, was true.   40

So after having paus'd a Little
Thought fit to swallow down his spittle
While Hermes, mounted on his Pinions
Returning sought his Sire's Dominions.
   The tidings spread at Pluto's bidding   45
The guests came posting to the wedding
In pairs the jovial crouds advance
For Pluto said he'd have a Dance
The reverend Judges left the Bench
And with him each had brought his wench   50
Old Charon found his Joynts grow supple
And brought his wife to make a couple
While Hecate, tho' in years so far gone
Yet footed it—with Demogorgon.

p. 104

The guilty found their pains suspended   55
And wish'd the mirth might ne'er be ended
The new adventure did so busy 'em
All Tartarus was turn'd Elysium.
Soon as the honey-moon was over
Thus to his Bride—the gloomy Lover   60
Address'd his speech 'The time, my Dear
Of losing thee is drawing near
The stars you know that gild our clime
Were never made to measure time
Fix'd to one point they still appear   65
Nor stir an Inch thro out the year
But, if I reckon with my Host
It can but want a week at most
The Loss will grieve me to the heart
But Jove commands—& we must part.   70
The week was gone; another came
But brought no Message for the Dame.

p. 105

The spouse began to yawn—amazing
Six months to be so long in passing
Another week he kept the woman   75
For time will mend his pace for no man

And then began to form suspicions
That Jove would break his own conditions.
And would not now the Dame recall
But let her stay for good and all   80
Now all his eloquence he broaches
In curses, railings, & reproaches
But troth he might as well forbear 'em
For Jove was too far off to hear 'em
At length the destin'd hour was come   85
Hermes was sent to fetch her home
Forth, by the heavenly convoy led
She left the regions of the dead
And Pluto felt, at parting with her
More joy than when he brought her thither. 90
Tis thus, in views of distant pleasure   p. 106
With eager hopes we court the treasure
But find it pall in the Possessing
And beg a riddance of the blessing.

Mr. Percy's Ode,   p. 107
On the Death of Augustus Earl of
Sussex;

And the Improvements design'd at Easton Mauduit.
Aug. 20: 1758
(he died Jan. 8 1758. Aetat. 30)

YE pleasing thickets, artless bow'rs,
    Fair remains of antient taste!
Whose winding paths, the vernal hours
    Once with every flowret grac'd!
Tho sad forsaken now ye lie,   5
Ye once could feast the smell, & charm the eye.

[W. S. has a footnote at the end of p. 107. It is badly charred and only
the words 'seriously ill (?)' are remaining. Percy adds the further note 'To
causes unknown. P.']

57

And, oft beneath your green retreat,
    Princely dames, & statesmen wise,
In solid merit nobly great,
    Shun'd the stare of publick eyes: 10
And in this lone retirement sought
The tranquil hour of *Freedom*, & of *Thought*

p. 108
But beauty is the sport of Fate;
    Soon it blossoms, fades & dies:
Where once the Graces smiling sate,   15
    Now in wild disorder rise
Unsightly Thorns; and brambles hide
Each lily-skirted path, the summer's pride.

Where woodbine's twin'd the silken wreath,
    Ivy twists it's balefull chain;   20
Where flow'rs diffus'd their fragrant breath
    Noisom weeds luxuriant reign
The smooth canal to Filth resigns
It's limpid Face, & ah no longer shines.

Ah sad reverse of former bloom!   25
    Fatal change of blissfull hours!—
Yet not for *ever* was the doom;
    Beauty will again be ours:
Thus sung the Genius of the wood,
All as beside the watery marge he stood.   30

p. 109
Forth from the thicket, lake & mead,
    Nymphs & Naiads round him throng;
And, spread in groups, with carefull heed,
    Mark the wonders of his song:
Young Fauns & Satyrs round him play,   35
Who thus in mystic strains resumes the Lay.

10 stare: glare [original reading, amended by W. S.]
  21 flowers: parks [original reading of W. S. heavily overscored by Percy and amended above line. Percy adds above the line a further variant: (or, Roses shed)]   24 ah: now [Percy's variant, above line]
  32 Naiads: Naids [W. S.'s original, corrected by Percy]

Gay smil'd the morn; & soaring high
   Hope, on golden pinions borne,
With glowing cheek & ardent eye,
   Hail'd our youthfull Lords return: 40
When after many a wistfull day,
To these glad scenes Augustus bent his way.

In thee, lov'd youth! we fondly view'd
   Rip'ning worth, & manly grace;
In thee, we said, will rise renew'd,   45
   All the glories of thy race:
In thee lost splendor to regain,
We fondly hop'd—but ah! that hope was vain

Wept ye, nymphs, that fatal day,   p. 110
   When the best of masters, friends,   50
In Life's fair blossom snatchd away,
   To the silent grave descends?
Ye wept—each vale & lonely shade
Witness'd your tears, the bitter moan ye made.

And ever shall the pensive mind,   55
   O'er the sad remembrance, bleed;
But now the mournfull wreath unbind,
   To a noble Pair succeed!
In this fair dame & generous Lord,
Behold your antient praise again restord.   60

See the future Plan they draw!
   Taste & elegance attend,
Each charm to heighten, veil each flaw,
   Neatness, beauty, grace to lend.
Art brings the Level and the Line,   65
While nature prompts & guides the whole Design.

38 borne: born [W. S.'s original, corrected by Percy]
40 youthfull: blooming [Percy adds variant above line]

Walls rush, & tortur'd yews expire;
   Bloomy shrubs unfold their dyes;
Dull avenues no longer tire;
   Lawns expand, & clumps arise;   70
New vistas catch the distant seat,
And every scene is beauteous, new, or great.

Blest Pair! may Love & Joy & Peace
   Waft you down the stream of time;
And when, at last, all these shall cease,   75
   Lead to mansions more sublime:
Then re-ascend a shining race
Heirs to your worth, & this high-favor'd Place.

Slander, or the Witch of Wokey

A Piece subobscurely printed by DR. HARRINGTON
of Wells, 1756

IN aunciente days, tradition showes,
A base and wicked elf arose
   The witch of wokey hight
Oft have I heard the fearfull tale
From Sue & Roger of the vale   5
   On some long winter's night.

Deep in the dreary dismal cell
Which seem'd, & was ycleped Hell
   This blue-ey'd hag was ty'd
Nine wicked elves, as legendes sayne   10
She chose, to form her guardian train
   And kennel near her side.

72 beauteous: striking [Percy's variant, below line]
77 ascend a: attend your [W. S.'s original, amended by Percy]
78 Ld. Augustus dy'd after 5 days illness of a Fever Jan: 8th 1758, aetat.
30, amid the most promising ⟨remainder charred⟩ [Footnote by W. S.]
[p. 112 blank]
9 blue-; blear [Percy's variant, above line]

Here schreeching owls oft make their nest
While wolves it's craggy sides possest
    Night-howling thro' the rock   15
No wholesom herb cou'd here be found
She blasted every plant around
    And blister'd every Flock.

Her haggard Face, so foul to see!   p. 114
Her mouth unmeet a mouth to be!   20
    Her eyne, of deadly Leer
She nought devis'd but neighbors' ill;
She wreak'd, on all, her wayward will
    And marr'd all goodly chear.

All in her Prime, have Poets sunge   25
No gaudy youth, gallante or younge
    E'er blest her longing arms
And hence arose her spight to vex
And blast the youth of either sex
    By Dint of hellish charms.   30

From Glaston came a lerned wight
Full bent to marr her fell despight
    And well he did I ween
Sich mischief never had been known;
And, since his mickle Lerninge shown,   35
    Sich mischief ne'er has been.

He chauntede out his godlie book   p. 115
He cross'd the water, bleste the brooke
    Then—Pater noster done
The gastly hag he sprinkled o'er   40
When Lo, where stood the Hag before
    Now stood a gastly stone.

Full well 'tis known adown the vale
Tho' strange indeed the doubtfull tale
   And doubtfull may appear   45
I'm bold to say there 's never a one
That has not seen the witch in stone
   With all her house-hold gear

But tho' this lernede Clerke did well
With grieved heart alas I tell   50
   She left this curse behind
That wokey-nymphs, forsaken quite
Tho' sense & beauty both unite
   Should find no Leman kind.

p. 116 Now Lo! ev'n as the Fiend did say   55
The sex have found it to this day
   That men are woundy scant
Here 's beauty, wit, & sense combin'd
With all that 's good & virtuous join'd
   Yet hardly one Gallante.   60

Shall then sich maids unpityed moan
They might as well like Her be stone
   As thus forsaken dwell
Since Glaston now can boast no Clerks
Come down from Oxenford ye sparks   65
   And Oh! revoke the spell.

Yet stay—nor thus despond ye Fair.
Virtue's the gods peculiar care
   I hear the gracious voice
Your sex shall soon be blest again   70
We only wait to find sich men
   As best deserve your choice.

44 doubtfull [Erased but legible]

Epitaph

p. 117

BENEATH, a sleeping infant lies;
   Who from his Parents rent,
Hereafter shall more glorious rise;
   Tho' not more innocent.

When the Arch-angels trump shall blow,   5
   And soul to Body join;
What crowds will wish their Life below
   Had been as short as thine?

                       Recd. From Mr. Percy

Song

p. 118

To the favourite Chorus in Atalanta

By ANTHONY WHISTLER Esq.

OH! let the various Force of sound
   Point out a Lover's anguish!
Now let the Notes with Life rebound
   Now let 'em sweetly languish.

Well may the Fife my Hopes declare;   5
Well may the Lute express despair;
Now let the notes with joy rebound,
Now let them sweetly languish.

Thus with my heart, if Silvia smile,
   Soon it exults with pleasure;   10
But if she frown, obedient still,
   That keeps a softer measure.

2 his: fond [Percy's marginal variant]
9 Recd. [Added by Percy, who thus repudiates authorship]
Title: [W. S. had written 'a favourite Chorus' but Percy firmly changed 'a' to 'the'. He also made one of his characteristic signs indicating a footnote, but no footnote appears—the bottom of the page is charred]

Then would ye with me sympathize,
Watch but the motion of her eyes;
Now let the Notes with Joy rebound,   15
Now let 'em sweetly languish.

p. 119

Strawberry-hill. A Ballad

By the EARL OF BATH

SOME cry up Gunnersbury
    For Sion some declare
Some say with Chiswick house
    No villa can compare
But ask the Beaux of Middlesex   5
    Who know the Country well
If Strawberry hill, if Strawberry hill
    Dont bear away the bell.

Some love to roll down Greenwich hill
    For this thing & for that   10
And some prefer sweet Marble-hill
    Tho sure tis something flat
Yet Marble hill, & Greenich hill
    If Kitty Clive* can tell
From Strawberry hill, from Strawberry hill   15
    Will never bear the Bell.

p. 120

Tho Surry boast it's Oatlands
    And Clermont kept so jim
And some prefer sweet Southcoats
    Tis but a dainty whim   20

1 Mr. Furnese's [W. S. in margin]
2 Ld Northumbd: [W. S. in margin]
3 Lord Burlington's [W. S. in margin]
7 Mr. Walpole's [W. S. in margin]
9 hill [Omitted by W. S.]
14 *She had a residence given her in the Demesne there [Percy's footnote]
15 First 'hill' omitted by W. S.
17 Ld. Linc: [W. S. in margin]
18 D. of New: [W. S. in Margin]

But ask the gallant Bristol
    Who doth in Taste excell
If Strawberry hill, if Strawberry hill
    Dont bear away the bell.

Since Denham sung of Coopers   25
    There 's not a Hill around
But what in Song or Ditty
    Is turn'd to fairy-ground
Ah peace be with their memory
    I wish them wonderous well   30
But Strawberry hill, but Strawberry hill
    Will ever bear the Bell.

Great William dwells at Windsor   p. 121
    As Edward did of old
And many a Gaul, & many a Scot   35
    Have found him full as bold
On lofty hills like Windsor
    Such heroes ought to dwell
But the little Folks on Strawberry-hill
    Like Strawberry hill* as well.   40

Hymn to Myra   p. 122

for the music of the slow air in Berenice

By Miss Wight

LET thy tears no longer flow—
Various is our Lot below!
Powr unseen will bring redress;
Droop not thus beneath distress;

---

21 Ld. Brist: [W. S. in margin]
40 *The seat of the Honble. Horace Walpole afterwds. Earl of Orford.
[Percy's footnote]

Look thro Faith, on scenes above,   5
Scenes of rapture, scenes of Love;
Where the child of grief is blest;
Where the weary meet with rest;
Let thy tears &c.
Tho' unpitied woes be thine   10
Thou wilt soon the Load resign:
See the smiling seraphs wait,
Prone to ease thee of the freight;
Prone to guide thy tearfull eye,
To the glorious tracts on high;   15
Hark what sound salutes thine ear—
Faithful servant! enter here,
Tho unpitied &c.

p. 123

Epigram

By Mr. Graves

THE wretch that courts the vulgar Great,
    And with Vulturio dines,
May gaze upon the sumptuous treat
    Nor ever taste his wines

There 's Burgundy, he lets you know;   5
    But quaffs the raisin's Juice:
His Claret's only bought for show,
    His muddy Port for use

3, 4 May never taste the sumptuous treat,
    Nor drink his costly wines. [W. S.'s variant in footnote]
3 sumptuous: costly [W. S.'s variant in margin]

On the Death of Mr. Pelham

By ANONYMOUS

p. 124

SAD solitary Mole! whose stream
    Thro' Lawns forsaken flows
Be witness to my falling tears
    And murmur back my woes.

Along thy banks no more the swain   5
    Shall sing his amorous tales
The voice of Joy no more be heard
    In Esher's mournfull vales.

Not all his virtues, all his Praise
    The great, the good can save;   10
Alas, Palemon, best of Men
    Lies mouldring in the grave.

In stately palaces o'er kings
    Relentless death prevails
Nor can we scape the fatal dart   15
    In Esher's peacefull vales.

Song by Col. Richard Lovelace, when imprison'd for the Cause of King Charles the I

p. 125

WHEN Love with unconfined wings
    Hovers within my gates;
And my divine Althea brings,
    To whisper at my grates;

16 Given me by Mr. Bridgens [Footnote by W. S.]

67

When I lie tangled in her Haire,   5
    And dazled with her eye;
No bird, that wantons wild in ayre,
    Enjoys more Liberty

When Linnet-like confined, I
    With shriller note shall sing   10
The mercy, goodness, majestye,
    And Glory, of my King;

When I shall voice aloud, how good
    He is; how great should be;
Not winds at large that curl the flood   15
    Enjoy more Liberty.

p. 126   When flowing cups run swiftly round
    With woe-allaying themes;
Our careless heads with roses crown'd,
    Our hearts, with loyal Flames   20

When thirsty souls in wine we steep;
    When Cups & Bowls go free;
No Fish, that tipples in the Deep,
    Enjoys more Liberty.

Stone walls do not a Prison make,   25
    Nor Iron bars a Cage;
The soul unstaind & innocent
    Calls this, an Hermitage.

If I, confined here, in Love
    And loyal thoughts, am free;   30
Angels alone that soare above
    Enjoy more Liberty.

8 more: such q. [W. S.'s marginal queried variant]
27 The soul: For souls q. [W. S.'s queried variant in margin]
32 From Mr. Percy's MS Collection of old Ballads [W.S.'s footnote]

An Old Song

(174 in the M.S. Collection)

As ye came from the holy Lande
  Of blessed Walsinghame,
O met you not with my true-Love,
  As by the way you came?

O how should I know thy true-Love,   5
  Who have met many a one,
(Returning from the holy Land)
  That have both come, & gone.

My love is neither pale nor browne,
  But as the Heaven's faire;   10
There 's none that hath *her* Form divine
  On either earth, or ayre.

Such a one did I meet, good sir;
  With most angelicke face;
Who did like Nymph or Queen appear,   15
  Both in her gait, & grace.

Yes—she hath left me all alone,   p. 129
  As tho' I were unknowne;
Who, sometime, loved me as herself;
  And called me, her owne.   20

What is the cause she leaves thee thus,
  And a new way doth take;
That sometime lov'd thee as herself;
  And thee, her Joy did make?

[p. 127 blank]
1 alterd [Percy's note above line, referring to whole poem]

69

I, that have lov'd her all my youth,   25
    Grow old, as now you see;
Love liketh not the falling fruite,
    Nor yet the withered tree.

For Love is like a careless childe,
    Forgetting promise past;   30
Deaf, dumb, & blind, whene'er he list,
    Nor ever firm, or fast*

p. 130   His vain desire is fickle found
    And yields a trustless Joy
Wonne with a world of toil & care   35
    And angerd with a toye.

p. 129   Such is the Love of woman-kinde,
    Or Love's blest *name*, abus'd;
Beneath* which, many vain desires
    And follyes are excusde   40

p. 130   But true-Love is a lasting Fire,
    Still burninge in the soul;
Which accident could never change,
    Nor time itself controul.

33–36 [This stanza appears at the end of the poem on p. 130 with a note:
'omitted.' An asterisk at l. 32 indicates the place of omission.]
40 [Supplied from Percy's Folio MS. Line charred off in Miscellany MS.]
41–44   (or rather)
            But true Love is a lasting Fire,
                That viewless *vestals tend;   *angels
            That burns for ever in the soul,
                And knows nor change, nor end.
[W. S.'s alternative final verse, in footnote]

The Boy and the Mantle

Retouch'd from Mr. Percy's M.S. Collection

'TWAS in the merry month of May,
 To †Carleile did repair
A wonderous little Boy;
 Of wisdom deep, and rare.

A gay and gorgeous mantle,   5
 This Boy had Him upon;
With brooches, ringes, & owches
 Full daintilye bedone.

He had a sute of silk,
 About his middle twin'd;   10
Yet gay attire he minded not
 Unless with manners join'd.

'God speed thee now, King Arthur,
 Thus feasting in thy bow'r!
And Guenever, thy goodlye Queen,   15
 Fair beauty's peerless flowr!

Ye Lords, & Lordlings in this hall,   p. 134
 I wish you all to heede,
Lest what you deeme a blooming rose,
 Should prove, a cankered weede.   20

Then, forthy, from his Potever
 Two wall-nut shells he drew;
And thence, a curious mantle
 Of wonderous Form, & hue.

[p. 131 blank]
1 alterd [Percy, above line, referring to whole poem]
2 †*Camilot* perhaps; that being the antient Palace of King Arthur. Mich:
Drayton, 142. [W. S.'s note on p. 132, which is otherwise blank]
4 wisdom deep and rare: wit beyond compare [W.S. in margin]

Here, have thou this, King Arthur,　　　25
　　Here have thou this of me;
And give it to thy comelye Queene,
　　All shapen—as you see.

It never shall become the wife
　　That once hath been to blame:　　30
Then every Knight in Arthur's court
　　Sly glaunced at his Dame.

Forth came Queene Guenever;
　　The mantle she assay'd:
The Ladye, tho' newfangled,　　35
　　Began to wax afraid.

p. 135 When she had tane the mantle,
　　And all therewith was cladde,
From top to toe it seemed
　　As tho' with sheers beshradde.　　40

One while it was too long;
　　Another while too short;
And wrinkl'd on her shoulders,
　　In most unseemlye sort.

Now green now red it seemed;　　45
　　Then all of sable hue;
Beshrew me, quoth King Arthur,
　　I think thou beest not true.

Down she threw the mantle,
　　With face all pale & wanne;
And sore disgrac'd & shamed,　　50
　　Unto her chamber ranne.

72

She curst the whoreson weaver,
  That had the mantle wroughte;
And bade a vengeance on his crowne,   55
  Who thither had it broughte.

I'd rather live in Deserts,   p. 136
  Beneathe a greenwood tree;
Than in King Arthur's bower,
  All shamed thus to be!   60

Sir Kay call'd forth his Ladye,
  And bade her to come neare,
Yet Dame, if thou be guiltye,
  I pray thee, hold thee there.

The Ladye, nothing daunted,   65
  Then came right boldlye on;
And now unto the mantle,
  Courageouslye is gone.

When she had tane the mantle,
  With purpose for to wear;   70
It shrunke up to her shoulders,
  And left her buttowke bare.

Then every merry Knight,
  That was in Arthur's court,
Gibed, & laugh'd, & shouted,   75
  To see that plesaunte sport.

Down she threw the mantle—   p. 137
  All chaunged was her Hue,
When with a Face of scarlette,
  She to her chamber flew.   80

53 weaver: walker [W. S.'s variant, in margin]
78 All: Sore [W. S.'s variant, in margin]

Then forth came an old Knight,
    A patteringe o'er his creede;
And proffer'd to the little boy,
    Ten nobles for his meede;

'And all the tide of Christmasse,   85
    Plumporrige shall be thine,
If thou wilt let my Ladye fair,
    In this thy mantle shine.'

But Little did his prayinge,
    Or Cunninge him bestedde;   90
She had no more hung on her,
    Than a tassel & a thread.

Then down she threw the mantle
    With
                                                      95

p. 138

Sir Craddocke call'd his Ladye,
    And bade her to come neere;
'Come winne this mantle, Ladye,
    'And do me Credit here: 100

'Come winne this mantle, Ladye;
    'For now it shall be thine,
'If thou hast never done amisse,
    'Since I first made thee mine.'

The Ladye, nothing daunted,   105
    Then came right boldly on;
And now unto the mantle,
    Courageouslye is gone.

When she had tane the mantle,
    And put it on her backe;   110
Within the Hemme it seemed
    To wrinkle, & to cracke.

94–96 [W. S. left incomplete. Percy did not attempt to fill the gap]

Lye still, she cryd, O Mantle!
 And shame not me for noughte:
I'll freely own whateer amiss   115
 Or blamefull, I have wroughte:

Once I kiss'd Sir Craddocke's mouth   p. 139
 Beneathe the green-wood tree;
Once I kiss'd Sir Craddocke's mouth,
 Before he married me!   120

When so she had her shreeven,
 And her worst fault had tolde;
The mantle all became her,
 Right comelye, as it sholde.

Most rich & fair of colour,   125
 Like gold it glittering shone;
Then all the Knights of Arthur's court
 Admir'd her, every one!

Thus while they stood admiring,
 The Boy look'd out of doore;   130
And where he chaunc'd to cast his eye,
 Was ware of a wild-boare.

He pulled out a wood-knife,
 And to the Boare he ran;
Struck off the boare's-head at a stroke 135
 And quitted him like a man.

Unto King Arthur's table,   p. 140
 The boares-head now is drawn;
Lo, there is never a Cuckolds knife
 Can carve this head of brawn.   140

122 her worst: all her [Marginal variant by W. S.]
129 Thus while: 2 1 [W. S. above line, indicating transposed order]

Then some their whittles rubbed
  On whetstone, & on Hone;
Some threw them under the table,
  And swore that they had none.

King Arthur & the little Boy   145
  Stood gazing on them then;
Lo all their whittle-edges
  Were turned back again.

Sir Craddocke had a Little knife
  Of steel & Iron made;   150
And, in a twinkling, thro the Necke,
  He drove the shining blade.

He drove the shining blade,
  Both easily & fast;
And every Knight in Arthur's court   155
                 taste.

p. 141 The Boy then held a wonderous horne,
  All golden was the Rimme,
Saith he, no Cuckold ever can
  Set mouth unto the brimme.   160

No Cuckold can this little horne
  Lift fairly to his head;
But, or on this side, or on that,
  He shall the Liquor shedde.

Some shedde it on their shoulder;   165
  Some shedde it on their thigh;
And he that coulde not hitt his mouth,
  Was sure to hitt his eye.

156 [Line partially charred]

76

Thus He, that was a Cuckold,
    Was known of every man—   170
But Craddocke lifted easily,
    And wonne the golden Canne.

Thus Horne, Boare's-head, & Mantle   p. 142
    Were His faire Ladye's meed;
And all such lovely Ladyes,   175
    God send them well to speede!

Yet Guenever, that wily Dame,
    With fell despight, coulde say,
Shee hath the wonderous mantle
    Borne wrongfully away.   180

See yonder shameless woman,
    That makes herself so cleane!
Yet from her Pillow taken
    Thrice five galantes I've seen

Priests, Clarks, & wedded men   185
    Have her lewd Pillow prest;
Yet she this gorgeous mantle
    Must bear from all the rest!

O then bespake the little boy,
    That kept the same in holde;   190
Chastise thy wife, king Arthur;
    Of speech she is too bold.

All frolicke light and wanton   p. 143
    She hath her carriage borne;
And given thee, for a kingly crown,   195
    To wear a cuckhold's Horn—

176 well: so q. [Marginal query by W. S.]
184 galantes: Leman [Marginal variant by W. S.]

Was none so oft in Arthur's court
 Had wrought the deed of shame;
Yet none so grudg'd the Mantle,
 To Craddocke's virtuous Dame.   200

p. 145

Edom of Gordon;

*From the Edition printed at Glasgow, corrected and enlarg'd by help
of Mr. Percy's old english M.S.*

1.

It fell out about Martin-mas,
 Quhen the wind blew schrile & cauld,
Said Edom o' Gordon to his men,
 We maun draw to a hauld.

2

And to what kind of hauld sall we,   5
 My merry men, repair?
We will gae to the house of the Rhodes
 To see that Lady fair.

3

Lo yonder appears the castle tall
 Those tours of antient Fame   10
And in them dwells a peerless dame
 Her Lord far gone frae hame.

4

The Ladye she stood on her Castle wall
 Beheld baith dale & down
And there she was ware of an host of men   15
 Came troopinge towards the town.

199 Yet none so grudg'd: A she that etc. [Variant by W. S. in footnote]
[p. 144 blank]
Title: [After the title Percy adds the note: 'The orig:']
1 fell out: happen'd [W.S.'s correction, in margin]
2 Quhen: When [Percy's variant, above line]

78

5

O! see you not, my merry men all,
　O see not you, what I see?
Methinketh I see an Hoast of men
　I muse, who they should be.　　　　　20

6

She deem'd it had been her lovely Lord
　All merrily prauncing hame
But it was the traitor Edom o' Gordon
　That reckt nae sin, nor shame.

7

She had nae sooner busket her sell　　　25
　Nor putten on her gown
Till Edom o' Gordon & his men
　Were round about the town.

8

They had nae sooner the supper sett
　Nae sooner said the grace　　　　　30
Till Edom o' Gordon & his men
　Were closed about the Place.

9

The Ladye ran up to her tower head
　As fast as she coud flee
To try if by her speeches fair　　　　35
　She could with him agree

27 Till: Ere [Percy's variant, above line]
29 the supper sett: laid the Cloth [Percy's variant, above line]
31 Till: Ere [Percy's variant, above line]
34 flee: drie [Percy's variant, above line]

10

As soon as he saw this Lady bright
And hir yates all locked fast
He fell into a rage of wrath
And his Look was all aghast. 40

11

Give owr thy house thou Lady gay
And thou sallt mine command
Give owr thy house, & eer sun-rise
Thoust be the Heyre o' my Land.

12

Come down to me, ye Lady fair, 45
And let me thy Bewtie see
This night ye's ly by my ain side
Tomorrow, my bride sall be.

p. 148 13

I winnae gi owr my house, she said,
Whoe'er sall make the claim; 50
Much less for traitorous Edom o' Gordon
Before my Lord come hame

14

I winnae come down, ye fals Gordon
I winnae come down to thee
I winnae forsake my ain dear Lord 55
That is sae far frae me.

41 owr: up [Percy's variant, above line]
42 thou sallt mine command: I will make thee a band [Percy's variant, above line]
43 owr: up [Percy's variant, above line]
45 ye: ze [so W. S. throughout, from Foulis. See Notes, p. 155]

15

Gi up your house, ye Lady fair;
  Gi up your house to me;
Or I will burn yoursel therein,
  Bot and your babies three   60

16

I winnae gie up thou fals Gordon
  To nae sik traitor as thee
Tho you should burn mysel therein
  Bot and my babies three

17   p. 149

But reach me my Pistol, Glaud, my man,   65
  Or deftly charge my gun
For unless I pierce this Bucher's hart
  My husband is undone.

18

She stood upon her castle wall,
  And let twa bullets flee;   70
But ah, they mist the traitor's hart,
  And only raz'd his knee.

19

Set fire to the house, quoth fals Gordon,
  Sin better may nae bee;
And I will burn hersel therein   75
  Bot and her babies three

60 Bot and your: And eke yr. [Percy's variant, below line]
64 Bot and: And eke [Percy's variant, below line]
65 But [Scored out in MS.]
66 deftly charge: charge you well [Percy's variant, above line]
68 husband is undone: Lord is all etc. [Marginal variant by W. S.]

20

And ein, wae worth ye Jock my man,
I paid ye well your fee,
Why pow ye out my ground-wa stane
Lets in the reek to me   80

21

And ein, wae worth ye Jock my man
I paid you well your hire,
Why pow ye out my ground-wa stane
To me lets in the Fire.

p. 150   22

Ye paid me well my Fee & Hire,   85
Sweet Ladie, I not deny;
But now I'm Edom o' Gordon's man
Maun either do, or die.

23

O then bespake her youngest child,
That sate on nurse's knee   90
My mother dear gie owre this house
For the reek it worries me.

24

I wold gie all my gold, my childe
So wold I, all my Fee
For one blast of the westerne winde   95
To blow this reek from thee

83 ground-wa [The hyphen was inserted by Percy]
85 Fee & Hire: Hire, Lade [Percy's variant, in margin]
86 Sweet Ladie, I not deny: You paid me well my Fee [Percy's variant, above
line]
96 from: frae [Percy's variant, above line]

25

But I mauna gie up my house, my dear
    To nae sik traitor as He
Cum weall, cum wae, my Jewells fair
    Ye maun take share wi me.   100

26

O then bespake her Dochter dear
    She was baith jimp & sma
O row me in a pair of sheets
    And tow me owre the wa

27

They row'd her in a pair of sheets   105
    And tow'd her owre the wa
But on the point of Edom's spear
    She gat a deadly Fa.

28

O bonny bonny was her mouth
    An chirry were her cheiks   110
And clear clear was hir yellow hair
    Whereon the reid bluid dreips.

29

Then wi his speir he turn'd her owr
    O gin hir face was wan
He said, you are the first that eer   115
    I wist alive again.

30

He turn'd her owr & ow'r again
    O gin her skin was white,
He said, I might ha spard thy Life
    To been some man's delight.   120

99 weall: well [W. S.'s reading, corrected by Percy]
104 And tow me owre [Supplied from Foulis edition. Line charred]

31

Busk & boon, my merry men all,
    For ill dooms I do guess—
I cannae behold that bonny Face
    That does the green-sward press.

p. 152

32

Them Luiks to freits, my master dear   125
    Then Freits will follow them
Let it neir be said brave Edom o' Gordon
    Was daunted by a Dame—

33

Now when this Ladye saw the Fire
    Come flaming oer her head   130
She lifted up her children twain—
    Ah me! my babes beene dead!

34

Thus Edom o' Gordon fir'd the House
    A sorrowfull sight to see
Now hath he burned this Lady fair   135
    Bot and her babies three

35

Now worde was brought to London-town,
    Whereas her husband lay,
That Edom o' Gordon had burnt his hall
    Bot and his Lady gay   140

128 by: with [Percy's variant, over line]
132 beene: been [W. S.'s reading, corrected by Percy, who adds a q. in the margin]
134 sight: sicht [Percy's variant, above line]
136, 137 Between these two lines Percy has added the sign 40⟩, indicating a preference for verse 40 (ll. 157–60) at this point.
137 town: the brave [W. S.'s variant, above line]

36

Soe hath he done his children three
   Each one more deare to Him
Than silver, gold, and Jewells were,
   Or his most precious Limb.

37

But when he luikt the Letter owre   145
   Good Lord! his hart was woe
Yes Edom o' Gordon, thy Life is mine
   Where'er thou ryde or goe.

38

Butte ye, bowne ye, my merry men all
   With tcmpcrcd swords of stcele   150
For 'till I have met with Edom o' Gordon
   My hart is nothing weele.

39

But when he came to Bitton's borrow,
   Sae lang e'er it was day;
They pray'd their Lord to litt & eat—   155
   But he maun gang away.

40

Now traiterous Edom was hors'd & gone
   Nae loitering at this tide
Nae place of safety there for him
   Or for his train to bide   160

141 Soe: Sae [Percy's variant, above line]
143 gold: gowd [Percy's variant, above line]
146 woe: wae [Percy's variant, above line] Good Lord: O then [W. S.'s
marginal variant]
148 goe: gae [Percy's variant, above line]
151 met with: found out [Percy's variant, above line. He adds the note: 'orig:']
153 Bitton's: Diacton's [Percy's correction, above line. He adds: 'orig;']
156, 157 [Percy adds a mark indicating the shift of verse 40.]
157 was: is [Percy's variant, above line]
160 train: Impes q. [W. S.'s queried variant, in margin]

41

He called up his merry men all
　And bade them haste away
For we have slain his children three
　Bot & his Lady gay

p. 154

42

O then he spied her ain dear Lord,　　165
　As he came owr the Lee,
Who saw his castle in a blaze;
　As far as he mought see.

43

Put on put on my mighty men
　As fast as ye can drie　　170
For he, that's hindmost of my train
　Sall neir get guid of me.

44

And some they raid, & some they ran
　Fu' fast out owr the plain
But lang lang e'er they sped frae hame　　175
　Baith Lady & babes were slain

45

Yet mony were the Mudie men
　Appeas'd thilk infant's claim;
For o' fifty men that Edom brought
　There were but five ged hame　　180

165 then he spied her [scored out in MS.]
169 mighty: michty [Percy's variant, above line]
177 men: lives [W. S.'s variant, above line; deleted by Percy]

46

A sacrifice of equal Price
　　Was offered to the Dame
And many were the Ladies fair
　　Lay Lemanless at hame.

47 p. 155

Then round & round the waes he went　　185
　　Their ashes for to view
At last he rushd into the Flames
　　And bade the world adieu.

From the Opera of Elisa: p. 157

sung *here* by M R. A R N O L D, Preb. of Worster. 1759

My fond shepherds of late were so blest,
　　The fair nymphs were so happy & gay,
That at night they went safely to rest;
　　And they merrily sang, thro' the day!

But ah! what a scene must appear! 5
　　Must the sweet rural pleasures be oer?
Must the tabor no more strike the ear?
　　Shall the dance on the green, be no more?

Must the Flocks from their pastures be led?
　　Must the herds go wild-straying abroad? 10
Shall the Looms be all stop'd in each shed?
　　And the ships be all moor'd in each road?

182 Was: Were [Percy's variant, above line]
187 he rushd into the Flames: into the Flames he fled [W.S.'s original reading, corrected by him]
177–84 [W. S. in the left margin indicates a re-ordering of the lines, thus: 1, 6, 7, 8, 5, 2, 3, 4.]
188 See a Similar Ballad pag. 223 [Footnote by Percy]
[p. 156 blank]
1–4 [Percy in the left margin re-orders these lines, thus: 2, 1, 4, 3.]

Must the arts be all scatter'd around,
   And shall Commerce grow sick of her tide?
Must religion expire on the ground,   15
   And shall virtue sink down by her side?

p. 159
The Mother;

By MISS WHITE of Edgbaston (Spenser's style)

BEHOLD with ardent Love, & pious care,
   The tender mother cast her eyes around;
Delighted with her prattling offspring fair,
   Where Field for sage instruction does abound
And much, I ween, she thinks of planting there,   5
Chaste virtue's favorite field—meet for such fruitage rare.

II

Kisses to One she gives with melting glee
   While to her throbbing heart another's prest
One little impe she places on her knee
   Upon her foot another takes his rest   10
Eftsoons her eyn the circling train survey,
To mark how Love & truth, in sweet assemblage play.

III

The lisping word, the supplicating eye,
   Full plain their various needment do declare
She kens their actions with a conscious joy   15
   And when she strives with kind maternal Care
p. 160 With smiles to cherish, or with frowns reprove
Tis aye with good Intent, tis aye with tenderest Love.

       [p. 158 blank]
       4 sage: much [Percy's variant, above line]

So views our heav'nly parent from on high
His frail creation with indulgent care 20
So does his hand each real want supply
Whether he grant, or he reject our pray'r
And, since each action well he can areed,
Certes, he once will grant to every Wight his need.

Song

p. 161

THE Parent bird, whose little nest
Is by her callow brood possest,
Beneath her warm & downy breast
    Does cherish them with Love:
But soon as time has plumd their wings, 5
And led them forth to groves & springs,
All unconcern'd the Parent Sings;
    Regardless, where they rove.

While hapless we of human race,
The lasting cares of Life embrace, 10
And still our fond affections place
    On what affords us pain
Tho' Children, as their years encrease
Obstruct our bliss, & spoil our peace
Our fondness, fated not to cease, 15
    For ever shall remain.

Song

p. 163

By MISS WHITE of Edgbaston, written in June, 1759

IN the winding recess of a vale,
    The lovely Amynta was found;
She wander'd her woes to bewail,
    Where the Aspin's all trembled around.

5 time has plumd: Nature plumes [W. S.'s variant, in footnote]
[p. 162 blank]

Where the plaint of the murmuring rills,   5
    Was heard, the green willows among;
While the zephyrs to neighbouring hills
    Thus wafted her heart-breaking song.

Let the winds whistle over my head;
    Let the night draw her curtains around;   10
Let Horror the vale over-spread;
    Yet the Hills with my woe shall resound:
But oh! may no *rival* be near,
    Whilst I my distresses recite;
The Malice of *Envy* I fear,   15
    Much more than the Horrors of night.

p. 164 What avails it that *once* I was gay;
    That the sweets of Contentment I knew;
That my sheep never wander'd astray;
    If my Shepherd, at last, is untrue?   20
When the Lasses so proudly enquire,
    And ask me my story to tell,
Far hence would I wish to retire;
    Far, far from such Pity, to dwell!

How could I with rigour deny?   25
    How could I, in pity, reprove?
'Twas late, eer I found with a sigh,
    That Pity was sister to Love.
Sweet sweet were the Flowrets of May;
    No season for doubt, & for spleen;   30
The Shepherd, as fair & as gay;
    And he call'd me, the Pride of the green.

24 such: their [W. S.'s marginal variant]
31 The: That [W. S.'s variant, in footnote on p. 165]

He talk'd of my shape & my air;   p. 165
    Recounted each several grace;
That the rose & the Lily so fair,   35
    Yet were blended more fair, in my face
That the Poppy, which glows in the Corn,
    With the Hue of my Lips could not vie;
Nor the dew-drop that hung on the Thorn,
    Cou'd not sparkle so bright as my eye   40

When first he from truth could depart,
    What sighs his false bosom would move!
Mean symptoms of *guilt* & of *art*,
    While, I dreamt, they proceeded from *Love*!
No more will I climb up these hills,   45
    The shades of the valley to view;
No more will I stray by the rills,
    Where he swore that his Passion was true.

Mean time, without blushes, the Swain   p. 166
    Can all his past triumph display;   50
Nor is there a nymph, will disdain
    To smile on a Shepherd so gay:
Yet why should the youth who deceives,
    From nymphs this encouragement find?
Or why should the maid he bereaves   55
    Of comfort, be treated unkind?

I weep, when I think how severe
    The maids of the village have been
Whene'er they behold me, they sneer;
    'Ay, there goes the Pride of the green'   60

34 several: beauty and [Percy's variant, above line]
43 Mean: They ⟨were⟩ [W. S.'s variant, in footnote on p. 165]

91

'This is she with whom none cou'd compare,
　'But ye Smiles, which once made her so gay,
'And the Graces that play'd in her air,
　'Are, like Damon, all vanish'd away'.

p. 167 But sure could they picture my woe,　　　　65
　Or guess at the pains I have felt,
Tho their eyes were of Lead, they wou'd flow;
　Tho their hearts were of Ice, they would melt:
If I ever did censure defy,
　If I ever did virtue offend,　　　　　　70
If Boldness e'er spoke in my eye,
　May I share the reproaches they tend.

But remember, ye fair-ones! be sure;
　E'er you thus on my weakness exclaim,
That it cannot *your virtue* secure,　　　　75
　To brand a poor maiden with shame.
Impute not to Folly, the Fears,
　That arise from a laudable pride;
She sought this recess for her tears
　Which she willingly wishes to hide.　　　80

p. 168 See the Rose-bud that courts the fresh gale
　All fearless it's beauty display
Should a mildew spread over the vale
　It shrinks & it withers away.
Since my woes cannot enter his ear　　　　85
　Since he 's false to the Lass o' the green
Since he treads the known haunts without Fear
　In those haunts I'll no longer be seen.

64 Are: Seem [Percy's variant, below line]
67 Lead: Flint [Percy's variant, above line]

A Pastoral

by the Same.

Soon as the morning, from her eastern bed
The smiling hours with rosy fingers led,
A gentle swain, whom Love deny'd to sleep,
From forth his osier fold, releas'd the sheep.
The Dams dispers'd around the valleys wide,   5
The snowy Lambs ran bleating by their side,
While, all beneath an oak, no longer gay,
Recounting o'er his woes, the shepherd lay.
    O love he cry'd, before I felt thy pain,
No happier peasant pip'd upon the plain!   10
While on this bank supine at ease I lay,
And sweetly carol'd all the summers day,
With what attentive ears, the rural throng
Stole to yon' thicket, to devour my song!
Of Love I sung, regardless of its dart;   15
Of Pains, I never dreamt would pierce my heart.
Then wayward Fancy led my thoughts astray,
O why was Reason, at the time, away!
Yet why should I sweet fancys deeds reprove
When wisdom joins, & Reason bids me love   20
How sweet the breeze, how kind are vernal show'rs
How soft the aromatic breath of Flowrs
Yet Phebe dear, can all their charms display
For she is fair & soft & sweet as they
To soothe my pain, perhaps the lovely maid   25
Could I but ask, would not refuse her aid
Can such a polish'd, such an heavenly mind
Be fair & sweet, be soft & yet unkind
Avert it Love—but ah when she appears
Revive 10,000 hopes, 10,000 fears   30

17 Then: Till [Percy's variant, above line]
28 sweet: coy [Percy's variant, above line]

Silent I stand, yet think the fair should heal
The latent wound, I never dare reveal.
Since first the pleasing torment I have known
My sheep run wild, so careless am I grown
And when my weather did the fields forsake   35
And led the flock into the thorny brake
I never strove the Lambkins to release
But let the brambles tear their snowy Fleece.

p. 171 Yet still my folds, a lovely prospect wear
My herds are healthfull, & my flocks are fair   40
No swain can boast a cottage more compleat
No dairy cooler, & no Pans so neat
Plenty of fruits my spreading vines afford
And golden apples crown my shining board
Nor let the stranger pine, my crops to see;   45
The weary stranger takes his rest with me.

O   Then why should Phebe treat me with disdain?
She knows full many a nymph upon the plain,
With me wou'd gladly take her future Lot
To reign the sovereign of so sweet a Cot   50
And Phebe prais'd it once—& smiling said
How sweetly, o'er the Porch, the wood-bine spread
How o'er the Lattice curl'd the teeming vine!
Grapes, honeysuckle; house & all be thine
For one kind word from Phebe's Lip, I cry'd;   55
I wont be sure but sure I think she sigh'd.

O   O mighty god of Love accept my prayr
O crown my passion, or remove my care
p. 172 A stately dome shall court thy aid divine
And myrtle thickets fence the sacred shrine   60
There shall the springs first opening buds appear
And autumns latest blossoms linger there.
Far from thy haunts be driv'n the vulgar crowd
The pert, the vain, the sordid & the proud

56 sure: yet [Percy's variant, above line]
62 And Autumns latest: There shall the etc. [Percy's variant, above line]

94

There the true Lover only pour his tears   65
Vent his fond hopes & undissembled fears
While for thy altar, every swain who loves
Shall breed six annual pair of milky doves—
My heart, O Love! has long been all thy own
—But make my Phebe bow beneath my throne   70
    But O! tis she my ravish'd eyes behold:
What streaming rays my heav'nly maid infold;
To kiss her feet, the smiling Flow'rs arise
And bud, & brighten where she turns her eyes
Happy the Plains where Phebe deigns to rove   75
But happiest he that merits Phebe's Love
What daring hopes my panting bosom fill
I fly to meet her on that wood-crown'd hill
Then if she smile, my tender care's I'll tell
But if she frown, my Love and Life farewell!   80

Song, by Lord Tyrawley: To Mrs. p. 173 Compton, the Consul of Lisbon's Lady, presenting him with a Cap, and Song

LAST night, as I was going to bed,
    I got your charming cap;
O could I wear it on my head,
    Reclin'd on your dear Lap!
This beauteous cap & you, my own,   5
I'd envy none that wears a crown.

But now, if I may be so bold,
    Pray how d'ye call this bonnet?
For that is neither sung nor told,
    In your diverting sonnet.   10

80 But if she frown [Reading conjectural. MS. charred]
5, 6 I'd show you that you stitch so true
    That I ⟨remainder charred⟩ [W. S.'s variant in footnote, p. 175.]

95

A *fuddling-cap* is lost on me;
A *Fool's-cap* ne'er could come from thee.

p. 174

If for *considering-cap* 'twas meant,
   Your caution I approve;
Your present too was kindly meant;   15
   I thank you for your Love:
In Politicians oft we find
Their caps with Loggerheads are lin'd.

Of Fortunatus it is said,
   He had a cap in store,   20
And, when he had it on his head,
   He was eclips'd all o'er;
O! such a cap as *that* I'd prize
To bring me where my charmer lies.

But now, to end this dolefull Ditty,   25
   Before it grows too long,
I must confess your cap was pretty,
   And charming was your song!
But if that you would hit me pat,
Dear Creature, lend me your old-hat.   30

p. 175

From the Chronicle Jan. 1759

ENCORE, Encore!
Mattei, once more
   That swelling note prolong!
While we attend
Th' harmonious End,   5
   New beauties close the song.

11 is: were q. [W. S.'s queried alternative, in margin]

Gilding the skies
The Rocket flies,
   Still towering to its height;
Then opens wide   10
His starry Pride,
   And fills the Air with Light.

A Romance p. 177

From the old Spanish History 'Las civiles Guerras de Granada',
attempted in the same numbers in English by Mr. Percy. *Río*
verde,* Río etc.

GENTLE River, Gentle River
   Lo thy streams are stain'd with gore
Many a brave & gallant captain
   Floats beside thy willow'd shore

All beside thy limpid waters   5
   All beside thy sands so bright
Moorish chiefs & christian warriours
   Join'd, in fierce & mortal Fight.

Lords & Dukes & noble Princes
   On thy fatal banks were slain   10
Fatal Banks that gave to slaughter
   All the Pride & Flow'r of Spain

There the Hero, brave Alonzo
   Full of wounds & glory dyd
There the fearless Urdiales   15
   Fell a victim by his side.

    [p. 176 blank]
    * green [W. S.'s footnote]

p. 178

Lo! where yonder Don Saavedra
   Thro' the squadrons slow retires
Proud Seville, his native City
   Proud Seville his worth admires.   20

Close behind, a Renegado
   Loudly shouts with taunting Cry
Yield thee, yield thee Don Saavedra
   Doest thou from the battle fly.

Well I know thee, haughty Christian   25
   Long I liv'd beneath thy roof
Oft I've in the Lists of glory
   Seen thee win the prize of proof.

Well I know thy aged Parents
   Well thy blooming bride I know   30
Sev'n long years I was thy Captive
   Sevn long years of pain & woe.

May our Prophet grant my wishes
   Haughty chief, thou shalt be mine
Thou shalt drink the Cup of Sorrow   35
   Which I drank when I was thine

p. 179

Like a Lion turns the warriour
   Back he darts an angry glare
Whizzing came the moorish Javelin
   Vainly spent amidst the Air.   40

Back the Hero, full of Fury
   Sent a deep & mortal wound
Instant sunk the Renegado
   Mute & breatheless on the ground

33 my: thy [W. S.'s reading, corrected by Percy]
36 Which [Conjectural. Page charred]
43 Renegado: Renegago [W. S.'s spelling at this point]

With a 1000 moors surrounded   45
    Brave Saavedra stands at Bay
Wearied out, yet never daunted
    Cold at length the warrior lay

Near him fighting, great Alonzo
    Stout, resists the Paynim bands;   50
From his slaughter'd steed dismounted
    Firm intrench'd, behind he stands.

Furious press the hostile squadrons
    Furious he repells their rage
Till by loss of blood infeebled;   55
    Who can war with 1000ds. wage.

Where yon Rock the plain o'er shadows   p. 180
    Close beneath it's Foot retir'd
Fainting sunk the bleeding Hero
    And without a groan expir'd   60

Chanson   p. 181

Assis sur l'Herbete
    Tyrsis, l'autre jour,
Dessus sa musette,
    Chantoit son amour;
'Cruelle Bergere,   5
    'Qui sçais tous charmer!
'Pourquoi sçais tu plaire,
    'Sans sçavoir aimer?

60 Renegado is properly an apostate; or one that denies the Faith—The
Spaniards use it for an infidel in general. [W. S.'s footnote to whole poem]

2

'Dessus cette Herbete,
  'Y a t'il un Berger,   10
'Qui soit moins volage?
  'Qui soit moins leger?
'Cruelle &c.

3

'Depuis que tes Charmes
  'Ont ravis mon Cœur,   15
'Je vis en allarmes;
  'Je tombe en Langueur;
'Cruelle &c.

4

p. 182

Cesse, cher Sylvandre,
  Le douce entretient;   20
Ton cœur est trop tendre;
  Je crains pour le mien:
A force d'entendre
  Que je puis charmer,
Je pourrois apprendre,   25
  Que je puis aimer.

5

Au bord du Rivage,
  Nous jouons tous deux;
Je t'offre pour gage
  Mes plus tendres Feux.   30
Aimable Bergere,
  Qui puis tous charmer!
Tu sçais plus que plaire;
  Car tu sçais aimer.

19 Sylvandre [Percy has written the final two letters above the line. W. S.'s script was not clear enough for him].

From the Chinese

By Mr. Percy

The Willow

SCARCE dawns the year—The Willow fair
With green invests her golden sprays
The Peach her inward spleen betrays
And bids the wind her blossoms tear
Bright Impe of Spring—what shrub shall dare 5
In gorgeous robe, with thee to vie
Thou wantst no Silkworm to supply
The lovelier Down thy branches bear.

SCARCE dawns the year—the willow covers oer
Her golden branches with a vest of green
The Peach eclips'd betrays her inward spleen
And sheds her slighted blossoms on the shore
Fair Impe of Spring! Let gorgeous Dyes no more   5
Presume with thy superior grace to vie,
Thou feedst no silkworm but thy Leaves supply
A lovelier down than ever silkworm wore.

2 Her yellow stem in green arrays
4 And lets her blossoms float in Air
   And gives her flow'rs to float in Air
5 Fair Child of Spring what specious glare
6 Shall with thy simple graces vie
[W. S.'s variants in footnotes. He misnumbered line 4 as 3]

2 With golden sprays assumes a robe of green
4 And sheds her blooms, & sickens at the thought
   And sheds her blasted flowers on the ground
[W. S.'s variants in footnote. He also wrote the word 'fraught' above his
variant for l. 2, evidently as a possible rhyme for 'thought' in a reconstructed
line 2]
5 —Let gorgeous Hues be taught
6 No more with &c.
8 —than ever silkworm wrought

Verses written in a garden,

By Lady MARY WORTLEY MONTAGUE;
communicated by MR. PERCY

SEE how that pair of billing Doves
With open murmurs own their Loves;
And, heedless of censorious eyes,
Persue their unpolluted Joys!
No Fears of future want molest   5
The downy quiet of their Nest;
No Interest join'd the happy pair,
Securely blest in Nature's care,
While her dear dictates they pursue—
For *Constancy* is *Nature* too.   10
Can all the Doctrine of our schools,
Our maxims, our religious rules,
Can Learning to our Lives ensure
Virtue so bright, or Joy so pure?
No—mark the great Creator's ends;   15
Where *Pleasure* still with *Virtue* blends:
In vain the Church and Court have tried
Th' united essence to divide:

The pedant Priest & giddy Rake
Discern alike their wild Mistake   20

The 5th. Ode of Horace,

by the Same

FOR whom are now those Airs put on?
And what new beauty's doom'd to be undone?

5 No: Nor [W. S.'s reading, corrected by Percy]
20 Shall find and own their wild mistake [W. S.'s variant in footnote]

2 And [Deleted by Percy]   new [Deleted by Percy]

That careless elegance of dress,
This Essence that perfumes the wind,
    Your every motion—must confess   5
Some secret conquest is design'd.

2

Alas! the poor unhappy maid,
To what a train of Ills betray'd?
    What Fears, what Pangs shall rend her breast?
How will her eye dissolve in tears   10
    That now with glowing Joy is blest;
Charm'd with the faithless vow she hears!

3

So the young sailor, on a Summer-sea,   p. 187
Gaily persues his destin'd way;
    Fearless and careless on the deck he stands;   15
Till sudden storms arise, & thunders roll:
    In vain he casts his eyes to distant Lands,
Distracting terror tears his timorous soul.

4

For Me, secure I view the raging main;
Past are my Dangers & forgott my pain;   20
    My votive Tablet in the temple shews
The Monument of Folly past;
    I paid the bounteous Gods my gratefull vows,
Who, snatching me from ruin, sav'd at last.

15 Fearless and: as [Percy's reading, above line. He deleted W. S.'s reading]
16 sudden [Deleted by Percy]
17 distant [Deleted by Percy]
18 timorous [Deleted by Percy]
19 For Me [Deleted by Percy]
20 Past are [Deleted by Percy]   Dangers: Dangers past o'er [Percy's variant, by insertion above line]
21 votive [Deleted by Percy]
23 bounteous [Deleted by Percy]
24 snatching me from ruin: sav'd me from the wreck [Percy's variant, above line]

Old Sir Simon the King,
from the M.S. Collection of Ballads

In a humour I was of late
As many good fellowes be
Who think of no matters of state
But to keep merry Company
That best might please my mind 5
So I rambled up & down
But Company none could I find
Till I came to the sign of the Crown
Mine Hostess was sick of the Mumps
Her mayd was fistle at ease 10
Mine Host was drunk in his Dumps
They all had but one disease
Says old Sir Simon the King etc.
With his Ale-dropped Hose
And his Malmsey Nose 15
With a Hey ding, ding a ding, Ding—

When I beheld this fight
I straight began to say,
If a Man be full o'er-night
He cannot get drunk to-day 20
And if his Drink he spare
He may hang himself say I
So may he mine Host, I swear
Therefore thus reason I

13 Says old Sir Simon the King,
   And young Sir Simon the Squire,
   Old Father Jenkinson kiss mother Wilkinson round about our coal fire
   Round about our Coal fire &
[Percy on p. 188, which is otherwise blank. This verse is the expansion of
W. S.'s 'etc.' It is incomplete owing to the charred page.]
13 Sir [Deleted by Percy].
17 Left blank by W. S. [Percy wrote in the whole line and initialed it 'P'.]
19 o'er-night [Supplied by Percy and initialed 'P'.]
21 he spare [Supplied by Percy and initialed 'P'.]
23 Host, I swear [Supplied by Percy and initialed 'P'.]

For Drink will make a man drunk   25
And Drunk will make a man dry
   And Dry will make a Man sicke
And Sicke will make a man dye
   Says old Sir Simon &c.

But when a mans drunk to-day   30 p. 191
   And laid in his grave to-morrow
Will any man dare to say
   That he dy'd for Care or Sorrow
But hang up all sorrow & Care
   It 's able to kill a Cat   35
And He that will drink till he stare
   Is never afear'd of That
For Drinking will make a man quaff
And quaffing will make a Man sing
And Singing will make a Man Laugh   40
And Laughing long Life will bring
Says old Sir Simon &c.

If a Puritan Skinker cry
   Dear Brother it is a Sin
To drink unless you be dry   45
   This Song I strait begin
   'A Puritan left his Cann
   And took him to his Jugg
And there he play'd the Man   p. 192
   As long as he could tugg   50

25 For: That [Percy's variant, above line]
26 Drunk will: Drunkenness [Percy's variant, above line]
27 Dry will: Dryness [Percy's variant, above line]
28 Sicke will: Sickeness [Percy's variant, above line]   a: as [W. S.'s mistake, corrected by Percy]
29 Sir [Deleted by Percy]
42 Sir [Deleted by Percy]

But when that He was spied
  He did neither swear nor rail
My only dear Brother he cry'd
  Truly all Flesh is frail
Says old Sir &c.   55

So Fellowes, if you be drunk
  Of Frailty it is a sin,
As it is to keep a Punk
  Or play at Out & In
For Drink & Dice & Drabbs   60
  Are all of this Condition
They will breed want & scabbs
  In spite of the Physician
But who fears every grasse
  Must never pipe in a meadow   65
And who loves a Pott & a Lass
  Must not cry—Oh, my Head! Oh.

1760

Verses written 30 years agoe

(From MR. PERCY)

BEHOLD the monarch-oaks, that rise
With lofty branches to the skies,
Have huge-proportion'd roots, which grow
With equal Longitude below—
Such is that fam'd mysterious tree   5
By mortals cleped, *Poetry*
Two Bards, who now in fashion reign,
Most aptly this device explain:

55 Sir [Deleted by Percy]
59 Out: In [W. S.'s variant, in margin]

106

If *this* with clouds & stars will venture,
That creeps as far beneath the Center.　　　10
More to explain the thing I mean,
Have you not, in a Saw-pit, seen
A skill'd mechanic, who has stood
On a fal'n pyramid of wood,
And hir'd a subterranean Friend,　　　15
To take his Iron by the end?
But which excell'd, was never found,
The Man above, or under, ground.
The moral is so pat and fit,　　　p. 194
That, were I but the God of wit,　　20
Then in a saw pit, in wet weather,
Should Young & Phillips work together

The best readings of the Following p. 195
Song, selected from 2 Copies in the
Tea-table Miscellany

THE sun was sunk beneath the Hill,
　　The western clouds were lin'd with gold;
The sky was clear; the winds were still;
　　The Flocks were pent within the Fold;
When, thro the silence of the grove,　　　5
Poor Damon thus despaired of Love!

2

Who seeks to pluck the fragrant rose
　　From the hard rock or oozy beach;
Who from each barren weed that grows,
　　Expects the grape or blooming Peach,　　10

22 work: saw [Percy's correction, above line]
(These Verses I found in MS in an old Table-Drawer in Lord Sussex'
Library. I have since seen them printed in one of Curl's Miscellanies intitled
Atterburyana &c. 12 mo. 1727, in this Book they are ascribed to *James Moore*
Esqr: the same, I presume, who afterwards took the name of *Smyth*; & who is
abused in the Dunciad. P.) [Percy's footnote]

With equal Faith, may hope to find
The truth of Love in Woman-kind.

3

No Flocks have I, nor fleecy care,
   No Fields that wave with golden grain;
No pastures green, or gardens fair,   15
   A Woman's venal heart to gain;
Then all in vain my sighs must prove;
For I alas—have nought but Love!

4

p. 196 How wretched is the *faithfull* youth
   Since women's hearts are bought and sold!   20
They ask no vows of sacred Truth;
   Whene'er they sigh, they sigh for gold.
Gold can the Frowns of scorn remove;
But I alas—have nought but Love!

5

To buy the Gems of India's Coast,   25
   What wealth what treasures can suffice?
But Indian gems could never boast
   The living Lustre of her eyes;
For these the *world* too cheap would prove;
While I alas—have nought but Love.   30

6

O Silvia—Since nor gems nor ore
   Can with your brighter Form compare,
Consider, that I offer more
   Than gold or gems—a heart sincere!
Let riches *meaner* beauties move;   35
Who pays thy worth, must pay in Love.

13 have I: I have [W. S.'s variant, in margin]
22 Whene'er: If e'er q. [W. S.'s queried variant, above line]

Percy's translation of the old Spanish
Romance Ensillenme el potro ruzio etc:

See page 56 of Civiles Guerras de Granada (Maurus loquitur)

SADDLE me my milk-white stallion,
    Saddle Him I won in fight;
Bring to me my moorish Targett
    Bring to me my Hauberk bright.

Tipt with steel of truest temper   5
    Bring to me my sturdy spear
Bring to me my Casque of Iron,
    Deadly dints on it appear.

With it bring my purple turban
    Richly deckt with feathers gay   10
Proudly nods the checquerd Plumage
    White & yellow, green & grey.

Now compleatly arm'd for battle
    Bring to me that scarf of Blue
Which the Fair Zelima gave me   15
    A sweet token to be true

Tell o tell my lovely mistress
    To look out & see me go
Go, to meet in mortal battle
    Proud Don Manuel my Foe.   20

Let her kindly smile upon me
    Let her cast one glance divine—
Slavery or death attend him
    Victory & Fame—be Mine.

        by Mr. Percy   25

23 attend him: shall end him [W. S.'s reading, scored through by Percy, who
inserts his correction above line]
    25 by Mr. Percy [Added by Percy]

A Sapphic of my old Friend Mr. Wren

Written by him 1733–4

TWAS underneath a Poplar shade
Poor Philomel her nest had made
Safely she deem'd might there be laid,
    There hatch'd, her Young.

But Strephon's eyes, oh savage swain!   5
Observd her toils; while all in vain
She warbled forth, in plaintive strain,
    Her piteous song.

All brutal rushing where she lay,
The caitiff seiz'd the little prey   10
And tore her callow joys away;
    He seiz'd, he tore!

For this she wept the night forlorn;
Her breast reclin'd against a thorn
That breast from whence her joys were torn   15
    Joys, now no more.

For ever ah for ever gone!
Sure Strephon had an heart of stone!
But soon shall he his sins bemoan,
    In piteous fashion;   20

p. 200   When to fair Celia he complains;
And scornfull she derides his pains—
Then shall he own, her melting strains
    Deserv'd compassion.

1 Corrected [Added by Percy above line, referring to whole poem]
7 in: her [W. S.'s original reading, corrected by him]
8 [Added by Percy over pencilled original]
11 tore: snatch'd [W. S.'s original, corrected by him below line]
14 Her: That [Percy's variant, above line]

Carmen encomiasticum, in Owenum Venedotiae principem. Auctore Gwalchmai, qui Floruit, 1100.

(Carmen originale verbum verbo Latinè redditum)

LAUDABO munificum, ex stirpe Roderici
Defensorem patriae, Dominum bonae indolis
Britanniae decus, agilem armisque expeditum Owenum
Rex qui nec recondit, nec cumulat nummos
   Tres classes venerunt, fluctus navigia,   5
Tres validae, primi ordinis classes, ut eum subito aggrederen-
   tur
Una ex Hibernia, Altera armatis instructa
Lochliniensibus (Danis) in undis longam seriam exhibens
Tertia trans mare venit ex Normannia
Cui fuit labor ingens et immanis   10
Et Draconis Monae proles (Oweni Filii) adeo in conflictu
   magnanima
Ut ibi fuerit magnus tumultus in eis impetuose adoriendis
Et ante eum, uti omnibus constat, fuerint confusio gravis
Strages, pugna, et mors honesta
Et bellum bellum cruentum et tremor tremor lamentabilis 15
Et circa Taly Moelfre mille vexilla
Et caedes caedes ardens hastarumque furor
Et festina festina cum indignatione Fuga et in undis Demersio
Et Menai absque refluxu ob sanguinis torrentem
Et color virorum sanguinis salsugine   20
Et lorica splendens, et vulneris dolor angens
Et mutilati prostrati ante principem rubrâ hasta conspicuum
Et Loegriae commotio et cum ea dimicatio
Et ejus in perplexitatem protrusio
Et exoriens gloria gladii victoriam reportantis   25
In linguis (gentibus) centum et quadringenta ad eum
Pro merito debiti laudandum.

19 sanguinis: sangunis [W. S.'s erroneous reading]

III

Four Copies of
Verses sent to me by J. C. from Mr.
Dilly Bookseller in the Poultry London,
for my opinion July 12, 1761

Latter part of the Third of Habakkuck paraphrased.

THO' the green blade desert the   meads
And withering blossoms hang the languid head;
Tho' the fair Fig-tree, thro untimely Frost,
It's ample leaf, its lusheous fruit have lost;
Tho' purple vines the raging whirlwind blast,   5
And Olives useless, on an heap, are cast;
Tho' struck by Death, the bleating Firstlings fall,
Vacant the Fold, untenanted the stall;
Yet still to Thee, Jehovah! pow'r supreme!
My God, my only Hope, my constant theme,   10
My strength, my song, my joy! alone to thee,
I pour the willing strain, & bend the knee.
O let thy Love with Firmness arm my breast
And guide my Feet, thro' Lifes rough paths,—to rest!

Inscription for an Hermitage

FOND man, to this sequesterd cell
Retire, & bid the world farewell
Ah, quit the city's noisy scene
For pleasures placid & serene:
To find within this lone recess   5
The rose-lip'd cherub, Happiness
That haunts the Hermit's mossy Floor
And simplest Peasant's humble door.
Fond man, how sweetly thou mayst spend
Thy blissfull days, nor fear thy end   10

Title. Mr. Dilly [The final letters of the name charred]
1 [left incomplete by W. S.]

Stealing thro' Life, as thro the plain
Yon Rill in silence seeks the main
Here when the saffron-vested Dawn
Spreads radiance o'er the dewy Lawn
For hours exempt from woe & sin   15
Thy ardent orisons begin
Here hail at Eve, that pow'r divine
Who made these tranquil moments thine.

Ode to Health   p. 205

NYMPH, that flies the crowded street
And the Satrap's lofty seat
Now a Dryad of the wood
Now a Naiad of the Flood
Goddess fair, & blythe & gay!   5
Health! accept thy votary's Lay
Not th' approach of Eve or Morn
Not the walk thro' waving Corn
Not the hills, & streams, & trees
Not the fragrant fanning breeze   10
Not the garden's pleasing scenes
Blooming Flow'rs, & varied greens
Sweet to smell & fair to sight
Yield one moment of delight
To the Wretch, who sighs for thee   15
Sighs for Health, or Liberty.
    Silvan maiden, blooming Fair
Hear thy constant votary's pray'r
From bleak hills & piny groves
Where the rude Norwegian roves   20
From Bermuda's radiant Isle
Where eternal Summer's smile
Come thro British valleys stray;   p. 206
Come, and make all Nature gay.

22 smile [Supplied from *Gentleman's Magazine* version. Page charred]

CONTENT, conduct me to thy Cell
Low in the solitary dell
Or on the side of some hoar hill
Near sheltering wood, or shaded rill.
Thee oft I met in H——'s vale   5
What time the tunefull Nightingale
Warbled her sweetly plaintive song
The beeches & the oaks among
On the fair banks of E——k reclin'd
Thy presence chear'd my drooping mind   10
Thy visits drove sad Care away
And made the Landskip doubly gay
How verdant then appear'd the trees
How soft & balmy was the breeze
How green how sweet the wood-bine bow'rs   15
How rich the scent of opening Flowrs
How bright the sun's enlivening beam
How smooth the polish'd limpid stream!
   Adieu lov'd plain & silver stream
Yet Thou, Content, be still my theme   20
p. 207 Thee smiling Fair, I woo again
Attend thy suppliants humble strain
O come from thy sequesterd cell
And deign once more with me to dwell.

From 'The Play-house to be lett', of Sir Wm. Davenant—To the Dance a-la-ronde

Mrs. Gosnel.
   AH Love is a delicate ting
   Ah Love &c.
   In vinter it give de new spring

---

11 Care: Cares [W. S.'s original reading, corrected by him]

Chor:

    It makes de dull dush for to dance
    Nimbell, as de monsr. of France   5

Mrs. Gosl.

    And dough it often does make
    And &c:
    De head of de Cuckold to ake

Chor:

    Yet let him bute vinke at de Lover
    And de paine it vill quickly be over   10

Mrs. Gos.

    De Husband must still vink a littel
    De husband &c:
    And some time be blinde as a beetel

Cho:

    Annd de Vife too sometime must be
    As errant a Beetel as he.   15

Written by Mrs. Pixell when very young   p. 208

From the French of M. des Barreaux

'Grand Dieu tes Jugemens' etc.

O THOU almighty being, just & wise
Who, crown'd with glory, rulest above the skies
Impartial judge, whose all-pervading sight
Detects the blackest crimes of darkest night
Behold me prostrate—Lo beneath thy throne   5
I sue for pardon, & my sins bemoan.
Mercy thy mild, thy best-lov'd angel send
To chase my terrors & my steps befriend—

4 dush [W. S.'s first reading, altered by him to 'dunsh'.]
5 France: Fraunce [W. S.'s original reading, corrected by him.]
15 Another there Stay Sir stay till the Constable waken [Footnote by W. S.]

But ah, my crimes so great, with room for grace
Will Justice yield her meek-ey'd rival, place?   10
I feel, I feel thy dreadfull vengeance rise—
Rush down the rocks, & hide me from his eyes
Oerwhelm me, waters; scorch me quick, O Fire
Annihilation—snatch me from his Ire.

    It cannot cannot be; th' almighty will   15
Ordains his wrath to punish, not to kill.
O! horror! see his red right hand extends
And hissing down, the vengefull brand descends
p. 209 Where can I fly, or how the rage endure,
Vengeance is His, & now he strikes secure   20
But ah my saviour's wounds my crimes atone
Justice & Love in mystic union shewn
The sacred mystery reveal'd in heav'n
The blest assurance to the world is given
Where can the thunder of his vengeance fall   25
But Christ's diffusive blood must quench the flaming Ball.

p. 211 # Verses by Miss Wheatley, to Mr. L——
on his desiring her to paint his Character

Decr. 13. 1760

THO' you flatter my Genius, & praise what I write,
Sure this whimsical task was imposed out of spite
Because this poor head, with much scratching & thinking,
Made some idle reflexions on rakeing & drinking,
To clip my weak wings—with malicious Intention—   5
You present me a theme—that defies all Invention.
Your Picture! Lord bless us—where can one begin?
To speak truth, were insipid—to lye were a Sin.

18 brand: bolt [W. S.'s variant in margin]
26 Memd. This was altered & corrected by me in many Places; & is, upon
the whole, rather a Paraphrase than a Translation. [W. S. in footnote.]

You might think me in Love, should I paint your perfections
Should I mimick your Faults, you might make—worse Ob-
    jections: 10
Should I blend, in one piece of superlative merit,
Good-nature, with wit; Condesension, with Spirit;
Should, with modesty, ease & goodnature be join'd;
Unlimited Freedom, with manners refin'd;
Courage, tenderness, honor, enthron'd in one heart;   15
With Frankness, Reserve; and with honesty, Art;
With these glaring good qualities placed in full view
Do you think any person could take it for you
Why then turn t'other side, says ill-nature; and find him   p. 212
In some few modish Faults, leave his sex all behind him;   20
For Levity, Flattr'y, & so forth, he 's famd:
Prithee, Patience—& let no such trifles be nam'd:
If his failings *be* such, time will certainly cure 'em;
And the Ladies—'*till* then—will with pleasure endure 'em.

To William Shenstone Esq;   p. 213
The production of half an hour's Leisure

Aug: 30, 1761

(Recd. by the Post, from an unknown Hand)

HEALTH to the bard, in Lezzo's happy groves
Health & sweet converse with the muse he loves
The humblest votary of the tunefull Nine
With trembling hand attempts her artless Line
In numbers, such as untaught Nature brings   5
As flow spontaneous like thy native springs.
But ah! what airy Forms around me rise
Bespangling these rude hills with various dyes

18 any Person could take it for you [Percy's reading, on p. 210, which is otherwise blank. Most of W. S.'s line is charred off, but it probably read as the
Annual Register version: any soul would believe it for you.]

In circling Dance a Pigmy crowd appear
And hark! an infant voice salutes my ear.   10
Mortal thy aim we know, thy task approve
His merit honour & his genius love
For Us what verdurous carpets has he spread
Where nightly we our mystic mazes tread
For us each shady grove, & rural seat;   15
His fallings streams & flowing numbers sweet
Didst thou not mark, amid the winding dell
What tunefull strains adorn our mossy Cell

p. 214
There every Fairy, of our sprightly train
Resort to bless the wood-land & the Plain   20
Beneath our feet unbidden beauties glow
The green turf brightens, & the Flowerets blow
There oft with thought sublime we bless the swain
Nor do we prompt, or he attend in vain.
Go, simple Rhimer, never shalt thou rue   25
The simple truth; go, bear this message true
Say to the Bard in Lezzo's happy groves
Whom Dryads honour & whom Fairies love
Content thyself no longer that thy Lays
By other's fosterd tend to Other's praise   30
Disclose each hoarded treasure of your Muse
Nor longer to the world such good refuse
Collect each scattered trophy of thy Fame
Worthy of Thee & thy much-honor'd name
Thy sense thy morals & thy verse can neer   35
In any better age than this appear
When Sense & virtue's cherish'd by the throne
And each illustrious privilege their own

p. 215
'Tho modest be thy gentle Muse, I ween,
'Oh lead her blushing from the humble green   40
'A fit attendant on Britannia's Queen'.
Ye sportive elves, as faithfull I relate

25 never shalt thou rue: bear this message true [Original reading, scored out
by W.S. and corrected by him above line.]

118

The intrusted mandates of your Fairy state
Visit these wilds again with nightly care
So shall my kine, of all the herd, repair   45
In healthfull plight to fill the copious pail
My sheep lie penn'd with safety in the dale
My Poultry fear no robber in the roost
My Linnen more than common whiteness boast.
Let Order, Peace, & Housewif'ry be mine   50
Shenstone, be genius, taste, & glory, Thine.

Cotswoldia.

Ballad by Mr. Marshall   p. 217

A young gent. of Dublin deceased—sent me by Mr. Hull.
Novr. 1761

THE Bells were heard all in the Morn,
    And Allen he rose full soon:
Sad tideings he heard for Allen to hear
    That Mary would wed 'ere noon.

Then Allen he call'd on Thomas's name   5
    And Thomas came at his call—
Make ready a Coffin & winding shroud,
    For Mary shall see my Fall.

When last we parted with brimfull eyne
    Right loveing she made a vow: 10
But Richard has twice as many sheep
    And Mary forgets me now.

50 orig: be taste & verse & Fame *still* thine
    be taste & fame & Fancy
    may fancy taste & Fame be   [W. S.'s footnotes.]
    p. 216 blank.

119

Then bear me to that grass-green bank
  Where we did kiss & play
And tell her the Rain that made it so green   15
  Has wash'd my Kisses away.

p. 218   The Bridegroom he led the Bride so fair
  The Parson he came anon—
But Thomas had brought his dear friends Corse
  Or ere the wedding was done.   20

He laid him on the grass-green bank
  Where they did kiss & play
And told her the rain that made it so green
  Had washed His kisses away.

When she beheld poor Allen's Corse   25
  Her maiden blush was lost
She faded, as on an April day
  A Primrose nipt by the Frost.

Then all beneath one fatal sod
  Together they buried were.   30
False Lovers who break your plighted vows
  Take heed ye come not there.

p. 219   Song

recd. at the same time

ONE april evening when the Sun
  Had journeyd down the sky
Sad Marianne with Looks of woe
  Walk'd forth, she knew not why—

4 she knew not why [Added by Percy. Left blank by W. S.]

Tears trickled down her faded cheek   5 p. 221
    Soft sighs her bosom heav'd;
Soft sighs reveald her inward woe
    Alas, she had been deceiv'd.

Ah, what a wretch am I become!   p. 219
    Ah, luckless Lass, cryd she!   10
The Cowslip & the violet blue
    Have now no charms for me.

This Little river when I dress'd
    Hath serv'd me for a glass
But now it only shews how Love   15
    Hath ruined this poor Face

What charms can happy Lucy boast
    To fix thy wavering Mind
What charms in Lucy more than Me
    Ingratefull! canst thou find?   20

Have you not told me 20 times,   p. 220
    You could not bear deceit
Ah who could think such harmless Looks
    Were form'd to hide a Cheat!

But now alas! too Late I find,   25
    Those Looks have me betrayd—
Yet I'll not waste my dying Hour
    Thy Falsehood to upbraid.

But what remaining Life I have
    I'll intercede with heav'n   30
That all thy broken vows to me
    At last may be forgiven.

5–8 [Omitted by W. S. at this point and copied out by him on p. 221 and
marked 'omitted'. A double caret between lines 4 and 5 indicates the omission.]

One one poor boon, before I dye
I would of Thee require
Ah! do not thou refuse to grant   35
A wretche's last desire.

p. 221
When you with Lucy shall appoint
The happy marriage day
O do not, over my grass-green grave
Inhuman! take thy way.   40

p. 223
Captain Carre*

A Fragment from Mr. Percy's Collection of old Ballads

**MASTER whither you will;
Whereas you like the best;
Unto the Castle of Bitton's-borrow
And there to take your rest.

But yonder stands a Castle faire   5
Is made of Lyme & Stone
Yonder is in it a faire Ladye
Her Lord is ridden & gone

The Ladye stood on her Castle walle
She looked up & downe   10
She was ware of an hoaste of Men
Came rydinge towards the towne.

See you not my merrye men all
And see you not what I see
Methinks I see an Hoaste of Men   15
I muse who they shoulde be.

39 not: not ye [W. S. scored out 'ye' as an error.]
* See p. 145 [Percy's note].
** This ballad and Edom of Gordon* seem founded on the same story; and it is possible to frame an admirable poem out of both. [Note by W. S. under title.]
16 shoulde be [Charred off in MS. Added by Percy on p. 222, which is otherwise blank.]

She thought it had beene her lovely Lorde p. 224
   He had come rydinge home
It was the traytor Captaine Carre
   The Lord of Westerton towne. 20

They had no sooner supper sette
   And after said the Grace
But the traytor Captaine Carre
   Was light about the Place.

Give over thy house thou Lady gay 25
   And I will make thee a band
All night within mine armes thoust lie
   Tomorrow be the heyre of my Lande

I'll not give over my house she said
   Neither for Ladd nor Man 30
Nor yet for traitor Captaine Carre
   Untill my Lord come home

But reach me my Pistoll * * * *
   And charge you well my Gunne
Ill shoote at the bloody Bucher 35
   The Lord of Westerton

She stood upon her Castle wall
   And let the Bullets flee p. 225
* * * She mist * * *

40

But then bespake the little Childe
   That sate on the nurses knee
Saies mother dear give oer this house
   For the smoke it smothers me.

I wolde give all my golde my Childe 45
   So wolde I doe all my Fee
For one blast of the westerne winde
   To blow the smoke from thee

40 about 9 or 10 stanzas wanting [Note by W. S. in text.]

But when she saw the Fier
  Come flaming on her head   50
She took then up her children two
  Sayes babes we all beene dead

But Adam then he fired the House
  A sorrowfull sight to see
Now hath he burned this Lady faire   55
  And eke her Children three.

p. 226

Then Captain Carre he rode away
  He staid no longer at that tide
He thought that place it was too warme
  Soe neere for to abide   60

He called unto his merry men all
  Bid them make haste away
For we have slaine his Children three
  All & his Ladye gay

Worde came to lovely London   65
  To London whereas her Lord lay
His castle & his hall were burned
  All and his Lady gay.

Soe hath he done his Children three
  More dearer unto him   70
Than either the silver or the Gold
  That men soe faine wold win.

But when he looks this writing on
  Lord in his hart he was woe
Sayes I will find thee Captain Carre   75
  Whether thou ride or goe

51 two [W. S. underlines and adds a q. in margin.]

Busse ye, bowne ye, my merry men all, p. 227
    With tempered swords of Steele
For 'till I have found out Captaine Carre
    My hart is nothing weele.   80

But when he came to Diactons* borrow
    Soe long ere it was day
And there he found him Captaine Carre
    That night he ment to stay**

On Gainsborough's Landskips with Portraits; p. 228
full length Figures, less than Life, drawn in
Pairs as walking thro' woods etc.

By Mr. Graves

To charm the soul, with equal Force conspire
The Painters Genius, & the Poet's Lyre.
When Milton sings, thro' Eden's blissfull groves,
With the first Pair, the ravish'd fancy roves;
Pursues each step, by various passions tost;   5
And quits with tears, the *Paradise* they *lost*—
Like that blest pair, by Gainsbrough's pencil drawn
See Nymphs & Shepherds range the flowery Lawn
We find the pleasing cheat, so well sustain'd
Each Landskip seems 'a *Paradise regain'd*'.   10

81 *same as Bittons before q. [W. S.'s query in margin. He underlines 'Diactons' in text.]
84 ** about 9 or 10 stanzas wanting. Quere on what original story these two Ballads were founded. [Footnotes by W. S.]
7 blest. first [W. S.'s original reading corrected above line.]
8 See. The [W. S.'s original reading, corrected above line.]
10 Orig. readings.
In Miltons fairy scene—When Milton paints the scene—our Fancy roves
With the first Pair—
We *trace* each step etc. The Nymps & swains etc.
Like that blest couple tread &c.
[Footnote by W. S. to whole poem.]

From the Cottager No. 13

Ode to the Sun

FOUNTAIN of heat & life, for they are One
Thou God of chill Idolatry! the Sun!
    What adversary blunts thy rays
    And pales thy noontide blaze
See motion from the restless water fled   5
And Nature in her winding-sheet lie dead.

II

O golden day-star! rise with wonted pow'r!
    To obstacles superior rise
Thy energy divine withhold no more
    But flame again thro' tepid skies   10
Unpetrify the ground, the streams unbind
    Restore the frozen human kind
Give my brisk blood in copious tides to roll
    And thaw this Icicle, my soul.

III

Blest had I been, if near to thee   15
Station'd in close-revolving Mercury
Sated with warmth but never cloy'd
Thy beatifick sight, I ever had enjoy'd!
Yet O! if ardent Piety
Can merit union with it's Deity   20
Me from this gelid Orb retrieve
And gracious Mithra, grant in thine to live.

There make each expanded sense
    With supernal Joys dispense
There my earth-born genius fit   25
    To converse with Solar wit

22 Mithra, grant in thine to live [Supplied from *The Cottager*. MS. charred.]

I'll there sustain with strengthen'd sight
The torrent of unceasing Light
   There thy Miracles explore
   Half a God, a man no more!   30

Irwan's Vale   p. 231

From Solyman and Almena

FAREWELL the Fields of Irwan's vale
   My infant years where Fancy led
And sooth'd me with the western gale
   Her wild dreams waving oer my head
While the blithe Blackbird told his tale   5
Farewel the fields of Irwan's vale

The Primrose on the Valley's side
   The green thyme on the mountains head
The wanton rose, the daisy pied
   The wildings blossom, blushing red   10
No longer I their sweets inhale
Farewell the sweets of Irwan's vale

How oft within yon' vacant shade
   Has Ev'ning clos'd my vacant eye
How oft along those banks Ive strayd   15
   And watch'd the wave that wanderd by
Full long shall I their Loss bewail
Farewell the sweets of Irwan's vale

Yet still within yon vacant grove   p. 232
   To mark the close of parting Day   20
Along yon flowery banks to rove
   And watch the wave that winds away
Fair Fancy sure shall never fail—
Tho' far from these & Irwan's vale.

10 blushing: blusing [So W. S. in error.]
19 Yet [Supplied from the *London Chronicle* text. Page charred.]

Sent me by Ned Cooky, as written by some Friend of his in Scotland

May 1762

I SAID, On the Banks of a stream
    I have pip'd for the shepherds too long
O grant me, ye muses, a theme
    Where Glory may brighten the Song
But Pan bade me stick to my strain   5
    Nor Lesson too lofty rehearse
Ambition befits not a swain
    And Phyllis loves pastoral verse.

II

The Rose with it's beautifull Red
    Looks wan by my Phyllis's bloom   10
The Breeze from the bean flowers bed
    To her breath, what a feeble perfume
The dew-drop so limpid & gay
    That loose on the violet lies,
Tho brighten'd by Phoebus's ray,   15
    Wants lustre, compared with her eyes.

III

A Lily I plucked in full Pride,
    Its freshness with Hers to compare;
And foolishly thought till I tried
    The flowret was equally fair   20
How Corydon could you mistake
    Your Fault be with sorrow confest—
You said that the swans on the Lake
    For softness might rival her breast.

While thus I ran on in her praise   25
  My Phyllis tript sportive along
Ye Poets! I covet no Bays—
  She smiles a reward for my song.
I find the God Pan in the right—
  No Fame, like the Fair one's applause   30
And Cupid must crown with delight
  The Shepherd that sings in his Cause.

Dooms-day   p. 235

ONCE, with a whirl of Thought opprest,
I sunk from Reverie, to rest—
An horrid vision seizd my Head:
I saw the Graves give up their dead;
Jove arm'd with terror burst the skies;   5
The thunder roars, the Lightning flies.
Confused, Amazed, it's Fate unknown
The world stands trembling at his throne
While each pale sinner hangs his head
Jove nodding shook the Heavn's & said   10
'Offending race of human kind
'By nature, custom, learning blind
'You who, thro *Frailty* slip'd aside
'And you who never fell, thro *Pride*;
'And you, by differing churches shamm'd   15
'Who come to see each other damn'd!
—So some Folks told you—but they knew
No more of Joves designs than you.

14 who [omitted by W. S.]

  The foregoing Verses were communicated to *Mr. Shenstone* by *Mr. Dodsley*, as
the Composition of *Dean Swift* . . . ⟨erasure of three lines⟩ . . . they are not con-
sistent with the Dean's known principles. P.

  The foregoing Verses are printed but very defectively in a publication of Mr.
Griffith's (author of The Letters from Henry to Frances) intitled The Friends
or Original Letters of a Person deceased. Lond. 1773 2 vol. 12. See page 77 of
Vol. 2nd, they are ascribd. to Dean Swift, in that Work. [Footnotes by Percy.]

The worlds mad business now is oer
And I resent those Pranks no more
p. 236 I to such Blockheads set my Wit!
I damn such Fools! Go, go youre bit.

p. 237
To Miss * * * * * on the Death of her Goldfish

Ah, dry those tears; they flow too fast—
His time was come! his Die was cast!
The shineing Fin, the golden scale
Alas you see could naught avail!
Nor Virtue's prayr, nor Beauty's pow'r,   5
Arrest his Fate, one single hour.
Fair Lady! moderate your grief
A Friend's advice may bring relief
Consider that we All must dye;
Your Fish—your Dog—your Cat—& I.   10
You'll not attend to what I'v said—
Your Peace is gone—your Fish is dead!
And shoud your Lover now draw near
And sigh, & call you all that 's dear
To tenderest sighs you'd answer—Pish   15
I hate mankind—I've lost my *Fish*.
I grant he was a Fish of merit
A Fish of Parts—a Fish of Spirit
p. 238 But sure *no* Fish should have the art
To captivate a Lady's heart.   20
Allow him every perfection
Yet still deny him your affection
Your Father'd swear you was undone—
He'd never bear a scaly Son
I'm very sure he ne'er would wish   25
To see his daughter suckle Fish

22 affection: subjection [W.S.'s variant in margin.]

130

And well indeed might take't in dudgeon
To be a Grandsire to a Gudgeon.
Your Sister too would make a Pother—
She'd never brook to call him Brother   30
Tis better far your Fish is dead
Than you should take him to your Bed
Your Mother never would abide
To see you lying side by side
Even you your self would think it odd   35
Should * * * stoop to kiss a Cod
Or asked her Fishmonger about
Some lovely, darling, amorous Trowt.
And swore no joy could eer be felt   p 239
While panting for her absent Smelt   40
Twou'd be most strange with streaming eye
To hear some tender Mother cry
Alas, my Child! poor thoughtless wench
Seduc'd, & ruin'd by—a Tench!
And now he swears he'll never marry   45
The Fright has made my girl miscarry
Cruel the Pangs we mothers feel
My Childs miscarried of an Eel
A Bird, a Beast, the mighty Jove
Became to gratify his Love   50
But you, O wonderful declare
A Fish is form'd to please the Fair
O could I but thy Favor win
Transform'd to Fish with golden Fin
I'd gladly swim the Little Lake   55
Confind in Bason for thy sake
Of to the surface raise my head
And from thy fingers nibble bread
In China or in earthen dish
I'd live & dye your faithful Fish   60
But since I've got no golden scale   p. 240
No shining Fin, no forky Tail

131

But arms & Legs, can speak & hear
I'm doom'd to languish & despair
With skin strippd off, no wriggling Eel   65
Expresses half the Pangs I feel.

Cambridge Decr. 26, 1757

p. 241 # By Mr. Horace Walpole, on Lord Granville

From the Chronicle Jan: 25th 1763

COMMANDING beauty smooth'd by chearful grace
Sate on the open Features of his Face
Bold was his language, rapid, glowing, strong,
And Science flow'd spontaneous from his tongue.
A Genius seizing systems, slighting rules   5
And void of gall with boundless scorn of Fools.
Ambition dealt her Flambeau to his hand
And Bacchus sprinkled fuel on the brand
His wish to councel monarchs or controul
His means, th' impetuous ardor of his soul.   10
For while his views outstript a mortal's span
Nor prudence drew, nor craft pursu'd the plan
Swift fell the scaffold of his airy pride
But slightly built diffus'd no ruin wide
Unhurt, undaunted, undisturbed he fell   15
Could laugh the same, & the same stories tell

66 Communicated to me by Miss Cotton—as read before to me, by Mr. Hickman—the author some of their acquaintance, but not mentioned—I guess, Mr. Meredyth. [Footnote by W. S.]

The Lines in the preceding Page were written a very few days before poor Mr. Shenstone's Death, & even after he began to droop; as appears from the Traces of the Letters, not so fair or legible as his usual writing. Being published in London, only 25th Jany. it could hardly reach Shenstone before the 27th & he died on the 11th February, 1763. P. [Note by Percy on p. 242, which is otherwise blank.]

And more a sage than he who bad await
His revels 'till his conquests were compleat
Our jovial statesman either sail unfurld
And drank his bottle, tho' he miss'd the world   20

    ⟨w⟩ent to Abington   p. 250
    High Sir Ho Sir
      went to Abington Ho
    There I met the widow Sanderson
      O she 's a dainty widow   5

    She did pull off my Boots
    High Sir etc.
    With many pretty Looks
    O she 's

    She has 3 candlesticks   10
    High Sir etc.
    With these 3 candlesticks
    She does play pretty tricks

    She did put me to bed
    With a fine Coverlid   15

    Did she come into bed
    Whether she did or no
    That 's not for you to know
    But she 's a dainty widow

Verses to be procur'd, and inserted in this Collection. 20
                                       p. 251
The Almahide of Lord B. (Chronicle 1759)
Doll Common
Baskerville's orig: M.S. by Swift and Pope.
Arthur a Bradeley

[pp. 243–9 blank.]
   1, 3 [Beginnings of lines charred.]
   1–19 [The widow poem is entirely Percy's addition.]
   22 I have it in an old miscellany [Percy's note below line. It may refer
to the 'widow' poem.]
   24 [Added by Percy.]

INDEX

[p. 252 blank.]
1–6 [Page-references charred.]
3 W——[Written by Percy over W. S.'s 'A——']
18 [Scored through by W. S.]
26 Epitaph: Epigrams [W. S.'s original reading, corrected by him.]
32 By Mr. Percy [Added by Percy.]

47 [Inserted by Percy.]
45–53 [Page-references charred.]
[pp. 256, 257 blank].

The Poem in p. 99 entitled Disappointment as written in 1752

MIRA, the toast of half our sex,
Whose blooming cheeks dame Venus decks
      With roses and with Lillies:
Who looks a Goddess, moves a Queen:
And if she sings, how clearly seen   5
      The Muses sweetest skill is?

Mira, as late I chanc'd to greet,
With looks, how affable and sweet?
      Return'd th' engaging creature
To day I ran to hail the fair: 10
But oh! how cold her looks and air?
      Scorn glow'd in every feature!

To learn whence all this sudden pride,
To Venus' shrine I warm applied
      And brib'd her with a sonnet;   15
Ah! simple! cry'd the laughing Queen
Mark yonder sky, how blue? serene?
      Dark clouds this Morn hung on it.

Know when she did her smiles bestow   p. 260
The Nymph had newly lost her beau   20
      But now the occassion varies
Think not from her a smile can fall
Who shone so late at Cynthio's ball
      'Mong Lords and Lady Maries

Then change your notes you witling Train   25
No more the *constant* Sex profane

By lik'ning to the Seas 'em :
They're formed you see by diff'rent Laws,
Since Fortune's chilling tempest thaws,
    And warmest sunshines freeze 'em.   30

1–30 [In an unidentified handwriting on pp. 259, 260 (original fly-leaf of MS.) The following leaf, pp. 261–2, is an extra leaf added by the binder, blank on both sides to which is pinned a cutting from the *St. James's Chronicle* with a text of Swift's 'Day of Judgement']

[The following pencilled notes appear in Percy's handwriting on the now charred original endpaper of the MS., which he has pinned inside the back cover:]

    Viva la Face viva l amor
    Viva sul' estiggiate
    Rende te a sposi un altro onor
    Viva la Pace ne due cor
    Viva etc.

  The following were printed in the Reliques
      p. 23. Gentle Herdsman
        113. Witch of Wokey
        125. Col. Lovelace
        128. Walsingham
        133. Boy and the Mantle
        145. Edom of Gordon
        177. Gentle River
            See also
  p. 223. Capt. Carre
    compared with p. 145 Edom etc.

NOTES

The following abbreviations are used for books frequently referred to:
Letters I—The Letters of William Shenstone, ed. M. Williams, 1939; Luxborough, *Letters—*Lady Luxborough, *Letters written by the late Right Honourable Lady Luxborough to William Shenstone, Esq.*, 1775; Hull, *Select Letters—*Thomas Hull, *Select Letters between the late Duchess of Somerset, Lady Luxborough, Miss Dolman, Mr. Whistler, Mr. R. Dodsley, William Shenstone, Esq., and others*, 1778; Graves, *Recollection—*Richard Graves, *Recollection of Some Particulars in the Life of the late William Shenstone, Esq.*, 1788; *Reliques—Reliques of Ancient English Poetry* by Thomas Percy, ed. Wheatley, 1927; Hales and Furnivall—*Bishop Percy's Folio Manuscript*, ed. Hales and Furnivall, 1867; Nic. *Ill.—*John Nichols, *Illustrations of the literary History of the Eighteenth Century*, 1817 ff.

Ode to a Fairy: Percy in a letter to Shenstone (B.M. Add. 28221, f. 14) identifies Mrs. Greville as having been Miss Meredyth—probably the friend of Lady Luxborough. Percy, usually extremely accurate, is in error. An obituary notice in the *European Magazine*, 1789, 763 has 'Mrs. Greville, authoress of an Ode to Indifference and wife of Fulk Greville, esq., formerly Miss Fanny Maccartney'. Fulke Greville was a friend of Dr. Burney, and his wife became Fanny Burney's godmother (*The Early Diary of Frances Burney*, ed. Ellis, 1907, i. 26). The Ode was published in the *London Magazine*, August 1761; *St. James' Chronicle*, April 1762; *Annual Register*, 1762, either under its present title or *A Prayer for Indifference* by 'A Lady of Quality'. It was first published in the *Edinburgh Chronicle*, 14–19 April 1759.

An Ode: This is the first of six of Miss White's poems. Percy's note in the Miscellany identifies her as the daughter of a Rector of Edgbaston and therefore a near neighbour of Shenstone. She married John Prynne Parkes Pixell (1725–84), who was in his turn Rector of Edgbaston from 1750 until his death. Both Pixells were versifiers. He had a poem in vol. v of Dodsley's *Collection*, probably submitted by Shenstone. None of his wife's poems seems to have been published, but he was more fortunate: Baskerville brought out in 1759 *A Collection of Songs with their Recitatives and Symphonies for the German Flute with a Thoroughbass for the Harpsichord by Mr Pixell.*

*Verses on Leaving * * * * in a Tempestuous Night*: This is the first of nine poems by Thomas Percy. They have all been scrupulously edited by the author. Originally this poem had been a mild love lyric written of his future wife, companion verses to his better-known *O Nancy, wilt thou go* *with me?* As transcribed by Shenstone the title had read (presumably) *Verses on leaving A——*. In Shenstone's own index the A is quite clear. The name in line 8 had doubtless been Annie or Nancy. By the time Percy came to edit his friend's manuscript, he was more shy of showing his feelings. In the Index, remembering that Worcester was the original scene of the poem, over the A he inked in heavily a W. In the title he replaced the A—— with a row of * * * * and erased the letters with such vigour that he left a hole in the paper. In line 8 the lady became a mere conventional 'Delia'.

Copies of the original poem had been sent to three of his friends, Shenstone, James Grainger, and his cousin Wm. Cleveland (cf. B.M. Add. 32333, ff. 19–20), and the Delia version (cf. A. C. C. Gaussen, *Percy, Poet and Prelate*, 17) was published in the *Grand Magazine of Universal Intelligence* in 1758. In Pickford's life of Percy, which is the preface to Furnival and Hales's edition of *Bishop Percy's Folio Manuscript*, the poem was printed as 'unpublished' with the erroneous date 1788, leading the author to draw somewhat fanciful conclusions on the nature of Percy's affections in the thirtieth year of his marriage.

For The Hermitage of John Ludford, Esq.: Thomas Warton (1728–90) while Professor of Poetry at Oxford was a visitor to the Leasowes in the summer of 1758. 'Mr. Thomas Warton was also here with Lord Donegal, and has since sent me his 'Inscriptions', which are rather too simple, even for *my* taste' (*Letters I*, 496). Apparently this Inscription was an exception. It was first published as *Inscription in a Hermitage, at Ansley-Hall, in Warwickshire* in Warton's *Poems*, 1777, where it is specially marked as 'never before printed'. The 1777 version contains an additional verse before the final verse of Shenstone's version. See *Gent. Mag.* 1815, 387.

Peytoe's Ghost: Richard Jago (1715–1781) was a lifelong friend of Shenstone. They were at school together in Solihull, together at Oxford, and in adult life not far distant; from 1737 Jago was curate and later vicar of Snitterfield in the south of Warwickshire. Shenstone acted as Jago's literary adviser and oversaw the manuscript of his *Edgehill*, which was published in 1767. Jago provided Shenstone with two of his poems for the Miscellany in response to a letter of 6 January 1759, which asked for 'any new copy of verses of your own, or of your friends' (*Letters I*, 503). *Peytoe's Ghost* was published in *Poems, Moral and Descriptive by the late Richard Jago*, 1784, a volume collected by Shenstone's neighbour, John Scott Hylton.

The 1784 volume notes that this was a complimentary poem to Jago's patron, Lord Willoughby de Broke; Craven was the Hon. William Craven of Wykin, later Lord Craven; Mordant was Sir Charles Mordaunt, Bt. As a ballad imitation it had an obvious appeal to Shenstone.

On the Death of Squire Christopher: John Wigson was a Warwickshire friend of Shenstone, son of John Wigson of Solihull. He matriculated at Oxford in April 1728, aged 17. The poem does not appear to have been published.

In a blank leaf of the Siris: Richard Graves (1715–1804) was a contemporary of Shenstone at Oxford and remained a lifelong friend. From 1748 he was Rector of Claverton, Bath, where Shenstone often visited. In his ninetieth year, more than forty years after Shenstone's death, Graves wrote of him (in *The Triflers*, 1806):

> Tho' ere life's *noon* his glass was run,
> Yet gained he endless fame,
> While on the eve of ninety-one,
> How worthless is *my* name.
>
> Yet known for Shenstone's friend, even I
> Am somewhat famous grown . . .

His *Columella; or the Distressed Anchoret*, 1779, was suggested by the life of Shenstone, and in 1788 he published in reply to Johnson's somewhat contemptuous life of Shenstone, *Recollection of Some Particulars in the Life of the late William Shenstone, Esq.* Graves, as can be seen from the age at which he wrote the verses above, was an indefatigable poet. Eleven of his poems appear in the Miscellany. *In a blank leaf of the Siris*, a neat comment on Bishop Berkeley's philosophy and views on tar-water, was published anonymously in *The Festoon*, 1766, 177, a collection of epigrams largely written by Graves himself. It was republished and acknowledged by the author in his *Euphrosyne or Amusements on the Road of Life*, 1776, 134. These later versions expand the poem to four verses without improving it.

A Parody of the speech of Jacques in Shakespear: This amusing 'seven ages of the parson' was published in a shorter version in Graves, *The Spiritual Quixote*, 1772, xi, iv.

From the old M.S.S. Collection of Ballads: This was Shenstone's first attempt at doctoring one of the ballads from Percy's Manuscript. He altered his original, but not to the extent that he was to do later with *The Boy and the Mantle*. Percy in 1759 (B.M. Add. 28221) sent Shenstone 'very large transcripts from my MS. Collection of Ballads'. On 9 August of the same year he specifically mentioned 'the Heardsman'. Shenstone clearly set to work on the transcript. In June he wrote, 'I had retouch'd and transcrib'd . . . *The Gentle Heardsman*', and in October, 'As to the Heardsman, I will indeed send you *my* additional readings if you still desire them' (cf. *Letters I*, 513, 517, 520, 532, 633). Except at one point Shenstone's retouching was confined to a few verbal changes—'but' in place of 'and' and the like. The exception was three verses (7–9) which' are so defective in the Folio Manuscript that Percy in the *Reliques* published what is his own reconstruction based on the few surviving words. Shenstone, unaware that Percy was working at his own version, composed

141

verses 7–9 (lines 25–36) of the Miscellany version. At a later date he copied Percy's reconstruction of the three verses in a footnote on p. 26, with an explanatory note. Percy's final version of the three verses as printed in the 1765 edition of the *Reliques* differs from Shenstone's transcript. Either Shenstone revised Percy or (as is more likely) Percy made further revisions. For the original text of the whole poem see Furnival and Hales, iii. 524. Percy's text is in *Reliques*, ii. 89–91.

Giles Collin; an old English Ballad: Shenstone's interest in the Ballad was not merely in Percy's Folio Manuscript. This ballad was not part of Percy's Folio. It does not appear to have been printed in the eighteenth century and Shenstone must have had a manuscript which is not now available. F. J. Child in *The English and Scottish Popular Ballads*, 1882, printed no fewer than five versions, all differing from one another and from Shenstone's (ii. 279–80; iii. 514–15; v. 225). Child derived his versions of *Giles Collin* (or *Lady Alice*) from nineteenth-century transcripts and editions. Shenstone's version is appreciably earlier than these and may well be the original form. He does not appear to have touched it up to any serious extent.

'Now this is the song the Brothers did sing': At this point Shenstone has torn a couple of sheets from the note-book. His index, however, he forgot to alter, and it appears that on the missing pages 29–32 of the note-book there were two further ballads, *A Ludicrous Old Ballad* and *George Ridley's Oven*. I suspect from the ballad which he allowed to remain that these two proved on revision to be too 'ludicrous' for the tone of the Miscellany. The four lines beginning 'Now this is the song the Brothers did sing' probably are the last four lines of a lost piece and may have no connexion with the poem that follows, *My Dog and I have learned a trick*.

Bagley-Wood, A Parody: No author has been traced for this poem. The precise notes by Shenstone and Percy do not entirely square with the ascertainable facts. Wintle, Warden of Merton 1734–50, was a Gloucestershire man, not a Scotchman, but as his speech is described as 'broad' the misapprehension is perhaps understandable. Strait, fellow of Merton, is almost certainly Richard Streat, who became a fellow in 1712 and who was still fellow in 1731 when he was presented with the mediety of Gamlingay rectory. There was no Mertonian fellow named Giles during Wintle's wardenship. The name (unless the whole incident is imaginary) may be a nickname. On the other hand, the twenty fellows and the constant disputes that Wintle had with them are authentic. Like many university stories, it is probably a compound of fact and apocryphal accretion. The poem is apparently unpublished.

An odd old Ballad: This is one of the many English songs that were orally preserved and transmitted. It was printed with its music in *Wit and Mirth or Pills to Purge Melancholy*, vi. 233–4, 1720, but the version there differs slightly from Shenstone's. Shenstone either had the song from another source, which may have been a singer or a manuscript, or (as is more likely) he made his own slight alterations to the *Wit and Mirth* version.

A Solution: Anthony Whistler (1714–54) of Whitchurch, Oxfordshire, was an Oxford contemporary of Shenstone (matriculated 1732) with whom, in spite of an unsuccessful visit to Whitchurch in 1750 recorded in full in Graves's *Recollection*, 150–2, he remained on friendly terms. Shenstone provided Dodsley with four of Whistler's poems for vols. iv and v of the *Collection* and included three of his poems in the Miscellany. Whistler's only published volume was *The Shuttlecock, An Heroic-Comical Poem*, 1736, a copy of which Shenstone provided for Lady Luxborough. (Luxborough, *Letters*, 69).

A Solution is one of a group of 'Riddle' poems that had for a time been a craze with Shenstone and his coterie, several of their riddles appearing in Dodsley's *Collection*, the *Gentleman's Magazine*, and elsewhere. During 1740–1 Shenstone 'was engaged in a poetical contest with some writers in the *Gentleman's Magazine*, against enigmas or riddles; in which controversy, as he was rather serious in the affair, he called in the assistance of Mr. Whistler, myself, and one or two more of his friends' (Graves, *Recollection*, 98). 'I return you my thanks', Shenstone wrote to Graves (*Letters I*, 20), 'most heartily, for the poetical resentment which you have shewn against my censurers, the Riddle-masters.' *Gentleman's Magazine*, 1740, 519, has a defence of the riddles by the editor advocating 'a moderate use of enigmas'. Shenstone at least felt that this enigma of Whistler was worth preserving.

Horace's 'donec gratus eram': 'I am concerned for the memory of my poor friend Whistler; and regret that his *better* pieces did not fall into my hands. I think that Dodsley, however, would have done him greater justice, had he inserted his translation of "Horace and Lydia". It is true, the translations of that Ode are out of number; but *his*, if I mistake not, had many beauties of its own' (Shenstone to Jago 1759, 22 Feb., *Letters I*, 427).

In both of the above Whistler poems Percy has added his own suggested readings.

Advice to a Preacher: Dr. John Byrom (1692–1763) was not one of the Leasowes group, and Shenstone does not even spell his name properly. Byrom, at one time a Fellow of Trinity College, Cambridge, settled in Manchester and became the inventor of the Universal English Shorthand. *Advice to a Preacher* appeared in *The London Chronicle*, 1759, 10 November, anonymously under the title, *Charge of the Right Reverend * * * Lord Bishop of * * * to the Clergy of his Diocese*. The *Chronicle* text differs slightly from Shenstone's as the following opening lines show:

> Brethren, by this my mind you'll know,
> Learn to pronounce your sermons *slow*;
> Give every word of a discourse
> Its proper time, and life, and force. . .

Byrom's poems were published in two volumes as *Miscellaneous Poems* at Manchester in 1773. This poem appears in vol. i, pp. 121–3, again with slight though unimportant alterations, except in the title which had become *Advice to the Rev. Messrs. H—— and H—— To Preach Slow.*

A Song, by Miss White. Mutual Sympathy: For Miss White (Mrs. Pixell) see p. 139. Unpublished.

Asteria in the Country To Calydore in Town: This interesting poem by Lady Luxborough has never been published, and Shenstone's transcript is almost certainly the only copy. Henrietta Knight, Lady Luxborough, was parted from her husband for a suspected indiscretion with a young parson, John Dalton. She was 'exiled' by him to the country residence of Barrels in Warwickshire, where she became friendly with the Leasowes literary group, becoming one of Shenstone's most regular correspondents. *Letters written by the late Right Honourable Lady Luxborough, to William Shenstone, Esq.* was published by Dodsley in 1775. Shenstone and Lady Luxborough visited one another's houses and each wrote complimentary verses for the other. Lady Luxborough's verses on the Leasowes, *Written at a Ferme Ornée, 7th August, 1749,* appeared in vol. iv of Dodsley's *Collection,* and when Shenstone departed from Barrels after a visit in February 1747–8 he carefully placed on the table a copy of his poem *On fair Asteria's blissful plains* (Luxborough, *Letters,* 7). The group of friends—'heroes' and 'princesses' to one another—adopted pastoral names to match the country-literary setting. Lady Luxborough was Asteria, Shenstone was Cynthio, William Somerville was old Eugenio, and Captain Outing, who acted as secretary for Lady Luxborough, was Calydore.

This poem is undoubtedly Lady Luxborough's 'Verses to Mr. Outing' mentioned by Shenstone in *Letters I,* 137–8 in May 1748. They were sent by her to Shenstone in April: 'He [Outing] might have happened to mention them to you, and as they are not worth the trouble of asking for, I prevent you, by sending them, and hope you will throw them in the fire when you have read them. . . . I am no *Poetess,* which reproachful name I would avoid' (Luxborough, *Letters,* 20). Shenstone replied: 'Your Ladyship's verses to Mr. Outing entirely convince me that both your Pow'r and *Will* to confer Honour, where you do not entirely disapprove, are as great as I can desire . . . if you wou'd shun the Character of a *Poetess* . . . you must never write in Heroic verse with half the Elegance you *do*' (*Letters I,* 137).

Lady Luxborough's letters of 1747–8 make it clear that after a summer with friends around her in Barrels she is spending a quiet winter. Outing is in London; Mrs. Meredyth ('Joannah') has gone to town with her family, including the 'two nymphs' Patty and Harriet; the 'Salopian Bard', Shenstone, has gone back to the Leasowes 'to scoop new windings for his floods'; the 'parish-priest' (almost certainly her neighbour Parson Hall who had been staying at Barrels) has finished his visit; and the 'chaplain' (probably her neighbour Parson Allen of Spernall, whose poem on urns follows immediately in the Miscellany) has paid a fleeting call. The allusions to European affairs, Cronstrom, Berg-op-Zoom, the 'peace at Aix', and the 'war in Zealand', confirm the date of the poem.

A Receipt for a modern Urn: The author, Parson Allen, was the incumbent of Spernall, a few miles from Barrels. He figures frequently in Lady Luxborough's letters. This is a satire, clearly taken in good part, on the enthusiasm of Lady Luxborough and Shenstone for urns and appropriate inscriptions. They were corresponding vigorously on the subject in 1748–9, and Shenstone's letter of 13 November 1749 (*Letters I*, 230) to her is an elaborate treatise on urns and their decoration, including drawings and detailed measurements. The reference to Sanderson Miller's pillar, a great column he had designed for Hagley Park, dates the poem about 1750–1. The poem has not been published.

Song, by Mr. Somerville. To Lady Luxborough: Shenstone completes this group with a poem to Asteria by their neighbour, William Somerville (1675–1742) of Edstone, Warwickshire. Somerville's other song to her, *As o'er Asteria's fields I rove*, was published in Dodsley's *Collection*, iv. 295. The author of *The Chase*, 1735, had been a great friend of both Shenstone and Lady Luxborough, and Shenstone wrote of him in March 1743–4 to Jago (*Letters I*, 87):

> But now, since old *Eugenio* dy'd—
> ·The chief of poets, and the pride . . .
> No more Asteria's smiles are seen!
> Adieu!—the sweets of Barel's-green!

This *Song* seems not to have been published and is presumably one of his 'little poems and impromptus', 'too trivial or too local for the press', which Lady Luxborough had in her possession (Luxborough, *Letters*, 365, 368).

Under M. Queen of Scots: The Rev. Robert Binnel (1716–63) of Shifnal, Shropshire, was an Oxford contemporary of Shenstone. He became Rector of Newport in Shropshire and so a near neighbour. See *Letters I*, 512, for a projected visit. He was a friend of Percy and nephew of Humphrey Pitt of Shifnal, in whose house Percy found the Ballad Manuscript. He was the author of *The Christian Strife, a Sermon*, 1751, but there is no record of his having published verse. There is a brief note on him in Nic. *Ill.* vii. 248. Unpublished.

Mr. Jago to Miss Fairfax: For Jago see p. 140. This poem was first published under the title *To a Lady* in Jago's *Poems, Moral and Descriptive*,

1784, 171–2. In the printed version, 'Lauretta', the heroine of Shenstone's text, has been eliminated and 'Stella' becomes the new heroine. The 1784 version is arranged in stanzas and expanded.

Written Oct: 1761: For Richard Graves see p. 141. This epigram on the coronation of George III was published several times in versions with slight and insignificant alterations: *Annual Register*, 1761, 218; *St. James' Chronicle*, 30 January 1762; *London Magazine*, 1762, 44; in each case without author's name. Graves published it again anonymously in his collection of epigrams *The Festoon*, 1766, 168. The first publication in which he acknowledged the authorship was *Euphrosyne*, 1776, 115.

An Abridgment of the University Verses to the Queen: For the marriage in 1761 of George III to his bride Charlotte, the University of Oxford prepared a magnificent folio volume, *Epithalamia Oxoniensia, sive Gratulationes in augustissimi Regis Georgii iii et illustrissimæ Principissæ Sophiæ Charlottæ nuptias auspicatissimas*, 1761. Oxford poets contributed in English, Latin, Greek, Arabic, Welsh and Hebrew. The custom of preparing fine volumes of loyal but trite flattery was soon to cease.

On Mr. Pitt's return to Bath, after his Resignation, 1761: Pitt's resignation in October 1761 caused great protest and indignation. The *Gentleman's Magazine* of November of that year had a group of epigrams on the subject, including that immediately following in the Miscellany. I can find no periodical publication of this epigram, perhaps because Graves preferred that following. He published this epigram anonymously in *The Festoon*, 1766, 168, and (as the acknowledged author) in *Euphrosyne*, 1776, 116.

On Mr. Pitt's Resignation. 1761. At the time of the coronation the largest jewel had fallen from the king's crown and, when shortly afterwards Pitt resigned, the parallel was obvious. This epigram was published immediately, in the *Gentleman's Magazine*, November 1761, 528 and in the *London Chronicle*, 31 October 1761. In both it is signed 'Middleham', which is possibly a pen-name.

In the scotch Manner: Shenstone's search for songs and ballads produced this quasi-Scottish song from his cousin, William Saunders, who was left a bequest in Shenstone's will: 'I give to my cousins John Sanders and William Sanders of Tardebrigge, one hundred pounds.' There is no record of its having been published.

Stella: A Pastoral Monody on the Death of Miss Yelverton: John Huckell (1729–71) after graduating at Oxford (B.A. 1751) received the living of Hounslow, Middlesex. He published *Avon* in 1758 and an *Epistle to David*

Garrick in 1769. This monody is apparently unpublished. Since Miss Yelverton was a relative of the Earl of Sussex, Percy's friend and patron from 1753 when he went to the living at Easton Mauduit, Shenstone probably derived the copy for this poem from Percy.

An Epitaph from Cheltenham Churchyard; Another, on Miss Forder: There is no reason to assume that these have been published in any form.

Horace, Book II. Ode the 12th: Shenstone clearly knew little of the author; even his Christian name was unknown to him. Lewis Bagot (1741–1802), a son of Sir Walter Bagot, Bt., matriculated at Oxford in 1757. He became a Student of Christ Church and was Dean of Christ Church 1777–83, later holding in succession the bishoprics of Bristol, Norwich, and St. Asaph. He contributed poetry to several Oxford volumes, including the *Epithalamia Oxoniensia* published on the occasion of George III's marriage in 1761. This translation of Horace (written when the author was at Westminster School) was apparently never published. For biographical notes see Nichols, *Anecdotes*, v. 630–2.

An Impromptu; to Seignior Francisco: John Scott Hylton (1726–93), a man of considerable means, came to reside at Lapall House, Halesowen, a short distance from the Leasowes, in 1753. He became a close friend of Shenstone, Lady Luxborough, and their circle, and shared their literary tastes. Shenstone supplied Dodsley with two of his poems for vols. iv and vi of the *Collection*. It is to Hylton that we owe the edition of Jago's poems in 1784 and the preservation of the manuscript of the Miscellany, which he sent to Percy in 1763; the original letter to Percy is bound in with the early pages of the Miscellany. This poem is apparently unpublished.

To the Memory of R. West of Pope's in Hertfordshire: This poem commemorates Thomas Gray's friend, Richard West (1716–42). He died at Pope's near Hatfield in Hertfordshire and is buried in Hatfield Church. The poem was published anonymously in the *London Magazine*, 1759, 388. Shenstone's reference to the *London Evening Post* is erroneous. The author (evidently unknown to Shenstone) was Thomas Ashton (1716–75), a member of the 'Quadruple Alliance' at Eton—Ashton, West, Gray, Walpole. Ashton sent copies to Walpole and Gray. Walpole transcribed it in a letter to Thomas Mann (see Toynbee, i. 248). Gray included it in his Commonplace Book, now in Pembroke College, Cambridge. This transcript was printed in D. C. Tovey, *Gray and his Friends*, 1890, 171–2. These texts differ only in single words from Shenstone's copy.

Epigram, 'At the Squire's long board': An unpublished epigram by Percy, who has added the date of composition, 1752. Shenstone had originally written in place of 'contracted' in line 3 another word, and added a note. Percy scraped out the note and Shenstone's variant and reinserted 'contracted' adding a note 'the original reading' and (to the whole epigram) the note 'A Parody of Pope's Epigram on Colly Cibber'. The Miscellany manuscript shows Percy's care in editing anything that he had written himself, even if it be only four lines.

Epigram, 'My Lord complains': Published by Graves in his collection of epigrams *The Festoon*, 1766, 39. This epigram by Pope, like the verses by Swift on p. 129, evidently circulated in manuscript for many years before it found its way into print. It was first published by Warburton in his notes to *The Dunciad*, 1751, iv. 132. Percy copied it into one of his (unpublished) note-books with the note 'Given me by Mr. Shenstone who had it from Dodsley' (B.M. Add. 32237, f. 200).

Epigram on the Proclamation of War. Graves apparently did not publish this epigram, perhaps because he had tried the same joke before. In *Euphrosyne*, 1777, 230, he published what is clearly an earlier version, which he dates 1744. This earlier version had been published anonymously in the *London Magazine*, 1762, 44.

War Proclaimed at Brentford, 1744.

Britain at length her wrath declares,
And fierce to meet the foe prepares.
Bellona mounts the iron car,
Grac'd with the implements of war.
*Augusta sounds the dread alarm   *London
And all the ports their gallies arm.
Bristol and York have heralds sent
Denouncing George's dire intent:
Nay, Brentford now proclaims defiance,
Let Bourbon tremble at th'alliance.

Song by William Penn: Shenstone's note explains his reason for including the poem. William Penn of Harborough Hall was his uncle. Unpublished.

Pembroke the simple to XtChurch the Ample: This Oxford epigram by Graves was published without author's name in *The Festoon*, 1766, 196, and re-printed as his own work in *Euphrosyne*, 1776, 269.

Mammas atque Tatas habet Afra: An adaptation by Graves of Martial, i. 101:

Mammas atque tatas habet Afra sed ipsa tatarum
Dici et mammarum maxima mamma potest.

Graves published his adaptation under the title *To an affected old Lady* in *Euphrosyne*, 1776, 163.

An Oeconomical Reflection: By Graves, apparently unpublished.

Yesterday: A poem by Dr. Nathaniel Cotton (1705–88) of St. Albans. Cotton had a companion poem *To-morrow* in vol. iv of Dodsley's *Collection*. His *Visions in Verse for the Entertainment and Instruction of Younger Minds* appeared in 1751 and went through numerous editions. His poetry was gathered together by Dodsley and published as *Pieces in Verse and Prose* in 1791, but Dodsley evidently had no knowledge of *Yesterday*. It had, however, been published anonymously in the *London Magazine*, 1752, 426.

Un Soneto de Cervantes: *A Celebrated Sonnet, from the Spanish of Cervantes*: Shenstone is shaky on Spanish, as on French. I have left his text untouched. The Miscellany contains three translations by Percy from the Spanish. Of these, *Gentle River* was printed in the *Reliques* (i. 334–7), and *Saddle me my milk-white stallion* (p. 109) was afterwards printed in discarded proof-sheets. His version of the 'Celebrated Sonnet' remained unpublished until it was included by D. Nichol Smith in 1932 in *Ancient Songs chiefly on Moorish Subjects*—the title given by Percy to a volume of translations from the Spanish which he planned in 1775 and abandoned when it was in proof. B.M. Add. 28221 for the years 1759–60 contains letters which Percy wrote to Shenstone on the subject of his Spanish translations. Four other manuscripts of this sonnet are known, one printed in *Ancient Songs* (MS. in the Bodleian Library), one in Percy's Journal in the British Museum, and two at Harvard. Percy has made one slight alteration in Shenstone's text. *Don Quixote*, i. 43.

The Disappointment: An unpublished lyric by Percy, who added the note 'Written about 1753' and at the end of the Miscellany (see p. 137) had copied another version as *The Poem in p. 99 entitled Disappointment as written in 1752*. Shenstone had noted at the end of the poem the words 'From [?] Mr. Percy'. Percy scraped out the word I read as 'From' and inked in 'by'; he was claiming it as indubitably his own.

Pluto and Proserpine: James Merrick (1720–69), a Fellow of Trinity College, Oxford, was a versatile minor poet. He published a translation of the Psalms in 1765 and contributed to Dodsley's *Collection* and to the *Gentleman's Magazine*. His light verse (as here) is better than his serious efforts. Shenstone writes of him: 'I have known a person of the truest genius take great Pains to translate a Poem, when with one tenth part of the Labour he could have compos'd a Poem ten times better. For instance Merrick & his Tryphiodorus' (*Letters I*, 552). The reference is to his *The Destruction of Troy*, 1739, which he translated from the Greek of Tryphiodorus when he was nineteen. *Pluto and Proserpine* (apparently unpublished) is a work of more maturity.

Mr. Percy's Ode on the Death of Augustus, Earl of Sussex: This unpublished poem has hitherto been known only from references in letters. Percy

149

pays tribute with some grace to both his old patron and his successor. Copies were sent in 1758 to Grainger and to Shenstone. Grainger acknowledged his copy: 'I am greatly obliged for the Ode you have sent me, as it has in it almost every one quality of a good lyric composition. . . . The encomium on your late noble Patron is not more pathetic, than that on his Successor is artfully delicate' (Grainger to Percy, 18 October 1758, cf. Nic. *Ill.*, vii. 267). Shenstone as usual took a more active part, and the exchange of letters in B.M. Add. 28221 shows that he modified and corrected the poem: 'I think your Elegy on Lord Sussex extremely easy and genteel. Pardon the Hints I have interlin'd, and only use what you approve of them' (*Letters I*, 499). Percy wrote back gratefully: 'If they [the verses] ever can be made tollerable, it will be owing to the hints you suggest' (B.M. Add. 28221, f. 14). Shenstone's final draft in the Miscellany was further revised by Percy in the course of his careful editing of his friend's manuscript.

Slander, or The Witch of Wokey: One of the several ballad imitations that Shenstone included (as did Percy) with his selection of the genuine ballads. Henry Harington (1727–1816), a descendant of the Elizabethan Sir John Harington, graduated B.A. at Oxford in 1749 and M.A. 1752. He became an M.D. in 1762, establishing himself at Wells as a physician. He retired to Bath in 1771, devoting his leisure to music, and published several volumes of songs and glees. His *Witch of Wokey* was an undergraduate production of which the author was not in later years particularly proud. Percy printed the poem in the *Reliques* (i. 325) and notes that it had been published in *Euthemia, or the Power of Harmony*, 1756. 'Dr. Harrington withheld his name till it could no longer be concealed.' It was later printed in Pearch's continuation of Dodsley's *Collection*, 1768, i. 133. Percy used Shenstone's version for the *Reliques*: 'The following copy was furnished by the late Mr. Shenstone, with some variations and corrections of his own . . . it was thought the reader of taste would wish to have the variations preserved' (*Reliques*, i. 325). In the Miscellany version Percy's pencil has not been idle either.

Epitaph, 'Beneath, a sleeping infant lies': This anonymous epitaph Shenstone noted as 'from Mr. Percy'. Percy made sure that the authorship should not be assigned to him by adding before Shenstone's note 'Recd.' (i.e. Received). Graves published the verses in a slightly different text in his collection of epigrams, *The Festoon*, 1766, 152.

Song, To the Favourite Chorus in Atalanta: Anthony Whistler's third and final contribution to the Miscellany. For Whistler see p. 143. In these verses he provided words for one of the choruses in Handel's opera *Atalanta*.

Strawberry Hill. A Ballad: Shenstone (cf. p. 159) would have regarded this as a song rather than a ballad, but both the subject and the form interested him. William Pulteney, Earl of Bath (1684–1764), though a bitter opponent of Sir Robert Walpole, whom he had incessantly attacked in his journal *The Craftsman*, surprised Horace Walpole by visiting Strawberry Hill in 1755 and even more by leaving a ballad to commemorate the visit. 'Can there be an odder revolution of things', wrote Horace, 'than that the printer of *The Craftsman* should live in a house of mine, and that the author of *The Craftsman* should write a panegyric on a house of mine?' Horace quoted the ballad in letters to Richard Bentley and George Montagu (Walpole, *Letters*, ed. Toynbee, iii. 321–4; ed. W. S. Lewis, ix. 169). It then consisted of two verses only, the first and third of Shenstone's version. Horace Walpole expanded the ballad to five verses—the full poem appears in the edition of his *Works*, 1798, ii. 513–14, with a note that 'the second, fourth, and fifth stanzas were added by Mr. W.' It was printed in the *Gentleman's Magazine*, April 1756, 192 and in *The London Chronicle*, 8–10 August 1758, No. 252, p. 129. Horace Walpole visited the Leasowes in the summer of 1762, about the time this part of the Miscellany was copied out (*Letters I*, 638), but the source of Shenstone's text is undoubtedly *The London Chronicle*, which at line 21 reads 'Bristol', as does the Miscellany text. The other texts have 'Bristow', and the 1798 edition has the note 'William Bristow, brother of the Countess of Buckingham, friend of Lord Bath, and a great pretender to taste'. Shenstone's marginal note 'Ld. Brist.' further increases the error. Otherwise his notes sufficiently identify the owners of the various country seats. 'Great William' at Windsor (line 33) was the Duke of Cumberland. Percy's note to line 40 has some importance in the history of the Miscellany manuscript. His reference to Horace Walpole as the Earl of Orford dates the note as not earlier than 1791. Percy was still making additions to the Miscellany MS. almost thirty years after he received it.

Hymn to Myra: By Miss White of Edgbaston. Shenstone spells her name 'Wight' here and in his Index (on p. 253 of the Miscellany). She is also 'Wight' in *Letters I*, 505, 654. Another set of words for the music of one of Handel's operas, *Berenice*.

Epigram, '*The wretch that courts the vulgar Great*': An epigram by Graves, published in an expanded version of three stanzas in his *Euphrosyne*, 1776, 86.

On the Death of Mr. Pelham: Shenstone marks the poem 'by anonymous' and it must so remain. There is no record of its having been published. From the date at which this part of the manuscript was copied it is probable that the subject is the Hon. James Pelham of Crowhurst, Sussex, whose death is recorded in the *Gentleman's Magazine*, October 27, 1761. Pelham for over forty years had been secretary to successive Lord Chamberlains and principal secretary to the late Prince of Wales.

Song, by Col. Richard Lovelace, 'When Love with unconfined wings': Shenstone's version of this well-known lyric was derived from Percy's Folio Manuscript (Furnivall and Hales, ii. 17). Percy published the poem in the *Reliques* (ii. 322) from *Lucasta*, 1649, collated with the Folio. Shenstone tried his hand at improving on the Folio Manuscript version. The following are the major changes by Shenstone: l. 6 dazled (fettered, Folio); l. 15 Not winds at large (the enlarged winds, Folio); l. 23 No fish that tipples (fishes that typle, Folio); l. 27 The soul unstained (the spotlesse soule, Folio); ll. 29, 30: Here Shenstone redrafted completely, reading:

> If I, confined here, in Love
> And loyal thoughts, am free

in place of the Folio:

> If I haue freedome in my loue
> & in my soule am free.

One cannot claim any merit in Shenstone's versions: they merely serve to show how with older poetry he assumed a considerable and, to modern editors, unwarranted editorial discretion.

An Old Song, 'As ye came from the holy Lande': Percy sent a transcript from the Folio of this ballad, 'Walsinghame', to Shenstone for his opinion on 15 January 1758 (B.M. Add. 28221, f. 11*b*). For the original text see Furnivall and Hales, iii. 471–2. Percy in the *Reliques* acknowledged Shenstone's share in the editing of this poem: 'The copy below was communicated to the Editor by the late Mr. Shenstone and corrected by him from an ancient copy, and supplied with a concluding stanza' (*Reliques*, ii. 101). If we can assume that the version in the Miscellany is the version that Percy received from Shenstone, it is clear that Percy made his own alterations both on the original Folio version and on Shenstone's copy. Percy noted on Shenstone's version in the Miscellany 'alterd', meaning presumably altered from the Folio original. Shenstone's alteration had a weakening effect on the ballad. He smoothed out the scansion to iambic regularity by inserting light words (O, yes, that, yet, &c.) at intervals. The following two verses of the original illustrate his method:

I haue loued her all my youth,   [I, that have lov'd, W.S.]
But now am old, as you see.   [Grow old, as now you see; W.S.]
Loue liketh not the ffalling ffruite
Nor the whithered tree.   [Nor yet the withered, W.S.]

For loue is like a carless child,
& fforgetts promise past: [Forgetting, W.S.]
He is blind, he is deaffe, when he list [Deaf, dumb, and blind whene'er he list, W.S.]
& infaith neuer ffast. [Nor ever firm, or fast, W.S.]

In these two verses Percy generally followed Shenstone, but in the last line he reads: 'His faith is never fast.' Percy amended his friend's amendments of the ballads. From an examination of Percy's own copy (in Harvard) of the earliest proofs of the *Reliques*, it is clear that he first printed substantially the Folio version. But the text he finally adopted and published in 1765 was mainly Shenstone's (cf. R. M. Baine, *Harvard Library Bulletin*, v, 2, 248).

Shenstone in the Miscellany version includes an alternative form of the last verse. Percy used the second of the two for the *Reliques*. Neither bears comparison with the original:

> But loue is a durabler ffyer
> in the mind euer Burninge,
> euer sicke, neuer dead, neuer cold,
> ffrom itt selfe neuer turninge.

Shenstone's 'vestals' (or 'angels' as his alternative suggests) are too Augustan for the simplicity of the ballad.

The Boy and the Mantle: A further ballad from the Folio Manuscript. See Furnivall and Hales, ii. 301–11 for the Folio version. Percy (*Reliques*, iii. 2) states that his text is 'printed verbatim from the old MS.' Shenstone gave this ballad more editorial attention than any of his other versions received. Whereas the other ballads in the Miscellany were modified in words and phrases, *The Boy and the Mantle* was rewritten verse by verse. Percy noted 'alterd' at the head of Shenstone's copy. The poem may have been included among the 'very large transcripts from my MS. Collection of Ballads' which Percy sent to Shenstone on 4 February 1759 (B.M. Add. 28221, f. 16). Shenstone wrote of the poem to Percy in November 1759 (*Letters I*, 532). He was still working at the poem as late as November 1762, when he wrote to Percy (*Letters I*, 634), 'You must dun me once more for "The Boy & the Mantle" and then it shall be ready.' By February he was dead, and Percy did not receive the amended version. This may in part account for the unusual publication in the *Reliques* of this poem as 'verbatim from the old MS.' Shenstone's revision should be compared with the original in Furnivall and Hales. The following sample verses give some idea of Shenstone's (very considerable) alterations:

Folio MS.	*Shenstone*
I tell you Lords in this hall,	Ye Lords, & Lordlings in this hall,
I hett you all heate,	I wish you all to heede,
except you be the more surer	Lest what you deeme a blooming rose,
is you for to dread.	Should prove, a cankered weede.
Shee threw downe the mantle	Down she threw the mantle—
that bright was of blee:	All chaunged was her Hue,
and ffast with a redd rudd	When with a face of scarlette
to her chamber can shee flee.	She to her chamber flew.

Some rubbed their kniues	Then some their whittles rubbed
vppon a whetstone;	On whetstone, & on Hone;
some threw them vnder the table,	Some threw them under the table,
& said they had none.	And swore that they had none.

Shenstone in the revision turned the ballad into a smoothly running regularized poem far removed from the original.

Edom of Gordon: The inclusion of this ballad, like that of *Giles Collin*, shows that Shenstone was by no means dependent solely on Percy for his ballad material. *Edom of Gordon* was sent by Percy to Shenstone in 1759 (cf. B.M. Add. 28221, 9 August 1759). Shenstone began on his leisurely task of 'retouching': 'Edom of Gordon, of which you desire a Copy, must receive great alteration towards the Close, before I can *endure* that you should see it' (to Percy, *Letters I*, 520). 'I had retouch'd and transcrib'd both Edom of Gordon and the Gentle Heardsman long before the arrival of your letter. The former I read to a Scotchman, who seem'd a good deal pleas'd with it' (to Percy, *Letters I*, 513). The Scotchman—could he have been his cousin William Saunders?—apparently put Shenstone on a new track. In 1761 he is writing to John McGowan, a 'Writer', or solicitor, in Edinburgh, asking for 'any old Scotch Ballads' (*Letters I*, 595-9). McGowan, who had already provided him with *The Gentle Shepherd*, apparently sent him the first published edition of *Edom of Gordon*, printed by Foulis of Glasgow in 1755. From this Shenstone with assistance from the Folio Manuscript proceeded to construct his text. He wrote to McGowan enthusiastically: 'He [Percy] shewed me an old ballad in his folio MS., under the name of Adam Carr: three parts in four coincide so much with your Edom of Gordon that the former name seems to me an odd corruption of the latter. His MS. will tend to enrich Edom of Gordon with two of the prettiest stanzas I ever saw' (*Letters I*, 598).

Shenstone copied *Captain Carre* (the only form of the ballad in the Folio Manuscript) into the Miscellany with only the slightest verbal changes (see p. 122). His version of *Edom of Gordon*, however, as his letters indicate, is considerably altered from the Foulis text of 1755. The Foulis text had 29 stanzas. By fusing the Foulis text with *Captain Carre* and adding from his own invention, Shenstone produced virtually a new ballad of 47 stanzas for his Miscellany. The following analysis shows his source for each stanza, the numbers referring to the stanzas of the Miscellany version (Captain Carre, C.; Foulis edition, F.; Shenstone's invention, W. S.):

1-2	.	.	F.	13	.	.	C.	33-39	.	.	C.
3	.	.	W. S.	14-16	.	.	F.	40-41	.	W. S.
4-6	.	.	C.	17-18	.	C.; W. S.	42-45	.	.	F.
				19-23	.	.	F.			
7-10	.	.	F.	24	.	.	W. S.	46	.	.	F.; W. S.
11	.	.	C.	25-32	.	.	F.	47	.	.	F.
12	.	F.; W. S.							

154

When Percy came to edit the ballad for the *Reliques*, he first printed the Foulis text, as his earliest proof sheets show (cf. R. M. Baine, 'Percy's Own Copy of the *Reliques*', *Harvard Library Bulletin*, v, 2, 249). When the Miscellany came into his hands he cancelled this first text and used the Miscellany copy as the foundation of his final version for the 1765 *Reliques*. His deference to his friend's taste was considerable. Apart from four stanzas (3, 11, 13, 25) which he omitted, he accepted in their order the first 33 stanzas of Shenstone's conflated version. The verbal changes he allowed himself were mainly intended to keep the dialect more consistently Scots. But the ending of the ballad, the hero's suicide (alike in Foulis and Shenstone), displeased him, and the 36-stanza *Reliques* version concludes with seven stanzas almost entirely Percy's rewriting of both Foulis and Shenstone to give the hero a more heroic exit.

In view of all this, what did Percy mean when he added the note 'the orig.' to Shenstone's version in the Miscellany? Shenstone's ballad, as Percy knew, was very different from either of the originals, Foulis or Captain Carre. One could conclude that Percy added the note as an indication that the Miscellany version was *his* original, the form from which he derived his text for the *Reliques*. This is borne out in an unpublished letter of Percy to Sir David Dalrymple, 11 February 1764, where, in discussing his alterations to the poem, he makes an almost certain reference to the Miscellany Manuscript. 'I know not how far you will admit the alterations and enlargements: they were in some measure pointed out by my late friend Mr. Shenstone, who left among his papers some hints how and where he could wish the alterations might be made' (B.M. Add. 32331, f. 48). But 'the orig.' may only mean that Percy regarded *Edom of Gordon* as the 'original' in relation to the derivative *Captain Carre*. Shenstone followed the Foulis printing of 'zou', 'zour', &c. for 'you', 'your'. The typography is normalized in this edition, as it would have been in Baskerville's.

From the Opera of Elisa, 'My fond shepherds of late were so blest': All that Shenstone notes of this poem is that it was sung by Mr. Arnold of Worcester, 1759. Samuel Arnold, organist, of Worcester, was a young adherent of the Leasowes group. He set Jago's *Blackbirds* and a song by Shenstone to music (cf. *Letters I*, 72, 402). *Eliza, An English Opera* by Thomas Arne was published in 1757. The words were by R. Rolt and in the published version differ slightly from Shenstone's. This lyric with its music was published also in the *London Magazine*, 1757, 556.

The Mother: A further unpublished poem by Miss White of Edgbaston, somewhat influenced by Shenstone's own Spenserian *The Schoolmistress*.

Song, 'The Parent Bird': Another by Miss White.

Song, 'In the winding recess of a vale': Miss White again. This poem shows the influence of Shenstone's *Pastoral Ballad*.

A Pastoral: For Miss White see p. 139. These last three poems have not been published.

Song, by Lord Tyrawley: An unpublished poem by James O'Hara, second Lord Tyrawley, envoy-extraordinary to the Court of Portugal and later ambassador there 1721–44 and 1752–63.

From the Chronicle, 'Encore, Encore!' The Mattei of this poem is probably Filippo Mattei, who played in opera. Groves's *Dictionary of Music* records that he wrote an act in one of Handel's operas. Shenstone got the date of publication wrong. It was printed in *The London Chronicle*, 27–29 December 1759, No. 468, p. 620.

A Romance, 'Gentle River, Gentle River': Percy, in August 1759, wrote to Shenstone: 'To my Hoard of these [ballads] in our own Language I have added a small but curious Collection of old Spanish ones in a Spanish book entitled 'The Civil Wars of Granada' . . . I have ventured to send a Translation of one of them' (B.M. Add. 28221). When the correspondence that forms this collection came later into Percy's hands he added a note to the sentence: 'Probably that beginning Rio Verde, Rio Verde.' Shenstone replied in October (*Letters I*, 520): 'At present let me thank you for the Spanish Ballad . . . which is indeed a good one, and admirably well translated.' Percy included it in the *Reliques* (i. 335) and it was reprinted in *Ancient Songs*, ed. D. Nichol Smith. Shenstone's version differs only slightly from Percy's. There is a further MS. of the poem in Harvard.

Chanson: Shenstone sent this French pastoral to Percy in January 1760: 'Is it the *Tune* which makes me like this little French trifle, or has it any merit that can induce Mr. Percy to give it us in English?' (*Letters I*, 540). Shenstone's original draft of the poem for Percy is preserved in B.M. Add. 28221. There is no sign of a translation from Percy. Published in *Letters I*, 541–2. Shenstone's erroneous 'douce' in l. 20 is repeated in the B.M. copy—Shenstone's French was shaky.

From the Chinese, by Mr Percy: These two versions of the willow poem are variants of one of the several pieces of Chinese poetry which Percy translated from the French of P. J.-B. Du Halde's *Description Geographique, Historique . . . de l'Empire de la Chine*, Paris, 1735, and published as an appendix to his Chinese novel *Hau Kiou Choaan*, 1761. *The Eulogium on the Willow Tree* appears in vol. iv, p. 211 and is accompanied by a note on Chinese poetry, which Percy (in attempting 'the same kind of stanza with the original') says was composed 'in Quatrains or stanzas of four verses, the first and fourth, the second and third rhyme together'. Percy, ever anxious of Shenstone's advice, submitted to him two versions of the poem. Shenstone writes in November 1759: 'You have injoin'd me a very difficult Task in regard to the Willow-tree, especially if you lay me under that restraint, which you have observ'd yourself, in regard to the Rhimes. I own, I am not quite satisfy'd with either of the versions' (*Letters I,* 531). Shenstone copied both the 4xa and the 5xa version into the Miscellany and added variant readings of his own. For once Percy, in editing the manuscripts, leaves his own work untouched—perhaps because the finally printed form differed considerably from both versions. Compare

> Scarce dawns the genial year: its yellow sprays
> The sprightly willow cloaths in robes of green.
> Blushing with shame the gaudy peach is seen;
> She sheds her blossoms and with spleen decays.
> Soft harbinger of spring! What glowing rays,
> What colours with thy modest charms may vie?
> No silkworm decks thy shade; nor could supply
> The velvet down thy shining leaf displays.
> (*Hau Kiou Choaan,* 1761, iv. 211.)

Verses written in a Garden: These verses by Lady Mary Wortley Montagu were 'communicated by Mr. Percy'. They had been published in 1755 in vol. iv of Dodsley's *Collection* and were republished in the 1781 collected edition of her poems. See the following entry.

The 5th Ode of Horace: The second of Shenstone's two selections from Lady Mary Wortley Montagu. Published with the preceding poem in *The Poetical Works of the Right Honorable Lady M—y W—y M—e,* 1781.

Old Sir Simon the King: Shenstone reverts to the ballad. *Old Sir Simon* is in the Folio Manuscript but was not printed in the *Reliques.* It was printed by Furnivall and Hales in vol. iv, *Loose and Humorous Songs,* 124–7. The manuscript was defective mainly at the ends of lines and Percy filled in the gaps in the Folio Manuscript. When the Miscellany came into his hands, he filled out the defective lines with virtually the same text, adding from a source (which is not the Folio Manuscript), the new refrain. 'Fistle' (l. 10) is a dialect word meaning 'disturbed' or 'bustled'.

Verses written 30 years agoe: Percy's note ascribes this satire on Young and Ambrose Philips to James Moore Smythe. Shenstone had the copy from Percy, and B.M. Add. 28221 contains the letter and the copy which Percy sent in November 1760. Percy at f. 57 has added a note on the authorship similar to that he added to the Miscellany, and then goes on to suggest that if the poem were written in his own time two other names might be inserted in place of Young and Philips. Editing his letter at a later date, he deleted the two names so effectively that they are now illegible.

James Moore Smythe (1702–34) finds his place among the Dunces in *The Dunciad*, ii. 50; ed. Sutherland, 1943, 455, and elsewhere.

Lines 5 and 6 are Shenstone's addition to the Percy transcript.

Song from the Tea-table Miscellany: This Miscellany edited by Allan Ramsay appeared in four volumes from 1724 to 1740, and went through twelve editions in Shenstone's lifetime. The 'two copies' of the song are on pp. 139 and 395 of the edition of 1750. Shenstone generally followed the latter but—as always—introduced new readings.

'*Saddle me my milk-white stallion*': Percy submitted this translation from the Spanish to Shenstone on 27 November 1760 (cf. B.M. Add. 28221). Published in a slightly different text in *Ancient Songs*, ed. D. Nichol Smith, with the title *The Moor's Equipment*, the title that Percy gave it in the abandoned volume of 1775. There is also a manuscript at Harvard dated 'July 31. 1760'.

A Sapphic: '*Twas underneath a Poplar shade*': Christopher Wren of Wroxall Abbey, Warwickshire, the son of the architect, was an Oxford friend and a neighbour and 'old friend' of Shenstone. His son Thomas was on a visit to the Leasowes in the early summer of 1758 (cf. *Modern Language Review*, xlii. 423). Percy (whose knowledge of the minor verse of his friends is quite astonishing) adds the comment 'corrected'. A variant version—presumably that untouched by Shenstone—was published anonymously in the *London Magazine*, 1761, 214.

Carmen encomiasticum: This unpublished Latin version of an ancient Welsh poem is clearly what Shenstone referred to in his letter to Percy of September 1761: 'There was a little good-natured welch-man called upon me t'other Day. I think he said his name was Rice . . . he . . . left with me a little Welch Ode, with a literal translation of it in Latin' (*Letters I*, 591). Percy's reply is in B.M. Add. 28221 (October 1762), where he identifies the Welsh clergyman as Rice Williams, Rector of Weston, near Shifnal and Newport, Shropshire, and so another of the many neighbours who were ready to call on the Leasowes to admire the improvements and hand in a copy of verses to the owner.

The ultimate source of the ode was not Williams but a more learned Welsh parson, the Rev. Evan Evans, curate of Llanfair-Talyhaiarn in Denbighshire. Evans wrote to Percy 8 August 1761 enclosing the ode in Welsh and in Latin: 'I have received your kind letter inclosed in another from your friend Mr. Williams of Weston, for which I return you both thanks, and in order to make you some amends I have sent you an antient British Ode with a translation as literal as that wherewith the Greek poets are commonly rendred into Latin which was the way I was advised to translate them by a friend who wanted to send some by way of specimen to Mr. Gray' (B.M. Add. 32230, f. 16). Percy encouraged Evans and recommended him to Dodsley with the result that he published in 1764 *Some Specimens of the Poetry of the Antient Welsh Bards translated into English*. The Welsh original entitled *Arwyrain Owain Gwynedd* is printed on pp. 127–8. Evans's English version, *A Panegyric upon Owain Gwynedd*, is on pp. 25–26.

Thomas Gray adapted Evans's English version as *The Triumphs of Owen*. Once again Shenstone is close to the springs of romance.

Four Copies of Verses sent to me by J. C.: These four sets of verses solve the puzzles of *Letters I*, 593, where Shenstone writes to 'J.C.' on 17 Sept. 1761 offering criticism and suggestions in considerable detail on verses which he had submitted for Shenstone's commentary. The letter and the four verses together explain one another. 'J.C.' I identify as Joseph Cockfield, a biographical note on whom appears in Nic. *Ill.* v. 753–808. One of his poems printed in Nic. *Ill.* v. 779 is an *Inscription for an Hermitage* different from that submitted to Shenstone. Of the four poems the Habakkuk poem was published in the *Gentleman's Magazine*, 1760, 588, *Inscription for an Hermitage* in the *Christian Magazine*, 1761 (cf. Nic. *Ill.*, loc. cit.), and the *Ode to Health* in the *Gentleman's Magazine*, 1761, 87. The pair of Hermitage poems were printed in Fawkes's *Poetical Calender*, 1763, iv. 11, and vi. 9. All of Shenstone's versions incorporate the amendments he suggested in the letter to 'J.C.'

From 'The Play-house to be lett': This song, 'Ah Love is a delicate ting', is sung in broken English by Mrs. Gosnell at the end of Act II. First published in the Folio *The Works of Sir William Davenant*, 1673. Shenstone first copied 'dush' [= Dutch] in l. 4 as in Folio and later, probably not understanding the original, altered to 'dunsh' [= dunce].

Written by Mrs. Pixell, 'O thou almighty being': See p. 139 for Miss White (Mrs. Pixell). Shenstone has had a considerable hand in the version.

Verses by Miss Wheatley to Mr. L——: '*Tho' you flatter my Genius*': The verses of Miss Mary Wheatley (or Whateley) of Walsall came into Shenstone's hands in 1761: 'There has been deposited in my hands a large collection of Poetry, by a Miss Wheatly of Walsall; many of the pieces written in an excellent and truly classical style; simple, sentimental, harmonious, and more correct than I almost ever saw written by a lady' (to Graves, September 1761, *Letters I*, 588). These verses were published with slight variations in the text, but with the Mr. L—— of the title becoming Mr. S——, in the *Annual Register*, 1761, 247 (where by an error in copying they are ascribed to Miss Loggin), the text being taken from the

London Magazine, 1762, 46, which had appeared before the *Annual Register* for 1761. Her *Original Poems on Several Occasions*, 1764, 62, reprinted the poem, the shifting recipient now having become Mr. O——y·

To William Shenstone Esq., The Production of Half an Hour's Leisure: As Shenstone's note indicates, this poem arrived through the post and he had no knowledge of the author of the tribute. It was published in a revised text in the *Annual Register*, 1761, 246 and again in the *London Magazine*, 1762, 43. Shenstone showed his pleasure in a letter to Graves, September 1761: 'But nothing in the poetical way has pleased me better than a compliment, which I received about nine days ago by the post, under the feigned name *Cotswouldia*.—She must be some Gloucestershire lady that has seen the place. . . . It seems written by somebody of fashion by the style.—Can you form a conjecture?' (*Letters I*, 589, where she is identified as Elizabeth Amherst (1714–79), sister of Lord Amherst, and wife of Rev. John Thomas, Rector of Notgrove in Gloucestershire). 'She was celebrated for her poetical talent' is the note on her in Collins, *Peerage of England*, 1812, viii. 169. The poem was later included among the 'Verses to Mr. Shenstone' in *The Works of Shenstone*, 1764, ii. 376–8, and in *A Collection of the Most esteemed Pieces of Poetry*, 1767, 115–17.

Ballad by Mr. Marshall; *Song recd. at the same time*: These two poems by the same author are best annotated together. Shenstone's actor friend, Thomas Hull (1728–1808), provided him with copies of verses 'ever and anon' and *Letters I*, 584, 605, 607, 612 show Shenstone writing shrewd critical commentary on two sets of verses which he had received and which he distinguishes one as a ballad and the other as a song. The two poems referred to are those by Marshall, which he copied into the Miscellany. 'One of your Ballads,' he writes to Hull in 1761, 'is truly beautily [*sic*] and extremely proper to his [Percy's] purpose. It has that *Naiveté*, which is so very essential in Ballads of all Kind. As to the other . . . it is become habitual to me to call *that* a *Ballad* which describes or implies some *Action*; on the other hand, I term that a *Song*, which contains only an Expression of *Sentiment*. According to this Account, I believe one of your Pieces would appear a *Ballad*, and the other a *Song*' (*Letters I*, 613). Hull published the two poems in his *Select Letters*, 1778, ii. 139, 141. Shenstone evidently sent the Ballad to Percy, who printed it as the final poem in the earliest proofs of volume ii of the *Reliques* (cf. *Harvard Library Bulletin*, v, 2, 250). Later Percy changed his mind and dropped the ballad from the volume as finally published.

Captain Carre: Shenstone copied out this fragmentary ballad from the Folio Manuscript (Hales & Furnivall, i. 79–83) with no alteration beyond a slight modernizing of the spelling. See note on *Edom of Gordon*, p. 153, for Shenstone's fusion of the two poems.

On Gainsborough's Landskips: A further epigram by Graves. Published anonymously in a text slightly different from Shenstone's in the *London Chronicle*, June 1762, 607; and as Graves's acknowledged work in an expanded version in his *Euphrosyne*, 1776, 131–2.

From the Cottager No. 13; *Ode to the Sun*: Shenstone's note-book was now almost filled. From this point onwards he includes an unusually large number of poems copied not from manuscript but from the journals of the day. Of the remaining six pieces, three are taken directly from the *London Chronicle*. Shenstone perhaps was hastening to finish off the Miscellany in order to have it ready for Baskerville. 'The Cottager' was a miscellany series of essays and poems which ran in the *London Chronicle* from March 1761 to April 1762. This ode was printed in No. 43 (not 13 as Shenstone notes), 2–4 March 1762.

Irwan's Vale, from Solyman and Almena: This lyric by John Langhorne was printed in an 'Account of Solyman and Almena' in the *London Chronicle*, 18–20 March 1762, a few pages after the *Ode to the Sun*. It is virtually certain that Shenstone copied the poem direct from the *Chronicle*. The tale containing the poem had appeared at the beginning of the year.

Sent me by Ned Cooky: '*I said, On the Banks of a stream*': This is an imitation of Shenstone's own Pastoral Ballad. Edward Cooke (of Edinburgh) was a cousin of Shenstone. On Shenstone's death the Leasowes was bequeathed to another cousin, John Hodgetts, for life and on his decease to Edward Cooke (cf. *Notes and Queries*, 1867, xii. 289). Unpublished.

Dooms-day: This is an early text of the poem by Swift usually entitled *Day of Judgment*. See Harold Williams, *Poems of Swift*, 576. It was printed in *St. James's Chronicle*, 9–12 April 1774, but Percy, in his note in the Miscellany, states that the verses were printed, though defectively, in Richard Griffith's *The Friends, or Original Letters of a Person Deceased*, London, 1773, a rare book of which a copy is in Harvard. It is surprising how much of the poetry of even the greater writers of the period wandered around for many years in manuscript form and was printed, if at all, almost by accident. The Miscellany text is better than any other version and is clearly closer to Swift's original.

The note by Percy is illuminating. The first two sentences (signed P.) are in red ink, a medium he often used for his own notes on letters and documents. They were presumably written on his first examination of the Miscellany. The remainder of the note is in pencil, and the date 1773 shows that Percy is adding notes to the Miscellany ten years after he had received it from John Scott Hylton. A cutting from the 1774 *St. James's Chronicle* with the text of the poem has been pinned in (by Percy?) at the end of the Miscellany.

*To Miss * * * * on the Death of her Gold-fish*: Shenstone's note contains all that is known of this piece. Mr. Meredyth (guessed by Shenstone to be the author) would be the brother of the 'two nymphs' Patty and Harriet Meredyth of Lady Luxborough's poem on p. 31.

By Horace Walpole, on Lord Granville: Shenstone copied these verses, as he indicates, from the *London Chronicle*, 25 January 1763, 88. They formed his last entry in the Miscellany and Percy's note at the end of the poem rounds off the story of the Miscellany. From this point onwards its history belongs to Percy rather than to Shenstone.

Miscellaneous Entries: (*a*) Entries by Shenstone: At p. 251 of the Miscellany, Shenstone has made a list of three items 'to be procur'd, and inserted in this Collection'. *The Almahide* by Lord Bolingbroke, a long Pindaric Ode of over 250 lines, which Shenstone marked 'Chronicle 1759' does not appear in the *London Chronicle*. Shenstone's notes on his sources are not always accurate. *Doll Common* (to which he attached no source) was printed in the *London Chronicle*, 27 Feb.–1 March 1759, No. 339, p. 200. It is possible that he placed the note 'Chronicle 1759' against the wrong entry. His third entry, 'Baskerville's orig: M.S. by Swift and Pope', is a prize still undiscovered.

(*b*) Entries by Percy: After Shenstone's three entries on p. 251 Percy added '*Arthur a Bradeley*'. *The Ballad of Arthur of Bradeley* was printed on pp. 16–19 of *An Antidote against Melancholy*, 1661. On p. 250 of the Miscellany, left blank by Shenstone, Percy copied out in pencil a song *O she's a dainty widow*.

On pp. 259–60 there is an entry which may have been approved of by Percy, but which is not in his handwriting. An unidentified hand has transcribed his poem *Disappointment* (which Shenstone had already copied out on p. 99 of the Miscellany). This second text is noted 'as written in 1752'.

On the original end-paper of the note-book, which became detached but which was pinned to the new end-paper when Percy had the book rebound after the 1780 fire, Percy has made a list of those ballads in the Miscellany that he had included in the *Reliques*. The final scrap of Italian, which for no ascertainable reason he copied out (somewhat carelessly— e.g. 'Face' for 'Pace'), is from the libretto of Handel's *Atalanta*.

INDEX
of authors and entries in the Miscellany